"Shawn Lovejoy hits an important nerve with this challenging and insightful exposé of what real success in ministry looks like. Too often we've listened to the false gods of competition and numbers instead of to the Holy Spirit and Scripture. Shawn offers us needed corrective."

—*Larry Osborne, author and pastor of*
North Coast Church, Vista, CA

"Shawn has given us a book filled with practical insight. I wish I could have gathered this much wisdom in one book when I set out to start my first church seventeen years ago. I would have avoided so many painful mistakes."

—*Chris Seay, author of* A Place at the Table
and pastor of Ecclesia, Houston, TX

"Pastor Shawn Lovejoy is a great man of God who has translated a lifetime of ministry experience into practical wisdom. *The Measure of Our Success* will not disappoint any humble leader who desires to achieve their full potential in Christ."

—*Steven Furtick, lead pastor of Elevation Church,*
Charlotte, NC, and author of Sun Stand Still

"If anybody knows about what real success in the trenches of ministry and life looks like, it is Shawn Lovejoy. He's a fantastic leader and a person of character who everybody should be learning from!"

—*Jud Wilhite, pastor of Central Christian Church, Las Vegas*

"I wish I had this book when I started The Journey. Shawn diagnoses the problem and offers practical solutions for pastors who want to not simply survive but thrive in ministry for a lifetime. I highly recommend that everyone who serves in the church read *The Measure of Our Success* cover to cover."

—*Darrin Patrick, lead pastor of The Journey, St. Louis, MO,*
and author of For the City *and* Church Planter:
The Man, the Message, the Mission

"Real tools for real leaders. Shawn Lovejoy gets to the root of the problem and puts out an all-important call to pastors to radically alter our measure of success. The church is ready for this, and so am I! Are you?"

—*Pete Wilson, author of* Plan B *and senior pastor of Cross Point Church*

"Shawn is a practitioner with a passion for the church and her leaders. In *The Measure of Our Success*, Shawn speaks from his heart about taking a deeper dive into our motives and values as the church. He shares from his wealth of experience as a gifted leader."

—*Dave Gibbons, author of* XEALOTS: Defying the Gravity of Normality

"An encouraging must-read for any pastor feeling discouraged, worn out, and worried that success will never come."

—*Greg Surratt, founding pastor of Seacoast Church, Mt. Pleasant, SC*

"Finally a book from a pastor for pastors that confronts head-on the crap we all face. Shawn offers not just an assessment of the problem but practical advice on how to live differently going forward."

—*Tim Stevens, executive pastor of Granger Community Church, Granger, IN*

"Shawn Lovejoy is a gifted leader who tells the gutsy truth about pastors and leadership in *The Measure of Our Success*. In it he delivers practical insights for healthy and productive church leadership."

—*Dan Reiland, executive pastor of 12Stone Church and author of* Amplified Leadership

"This book will be a great tool for helping us trade in our own ideas of success in ministry for God's idea of success."

—*Matt Carter, pastor of preaching and vision, The Austin Stone Community Church*

THE MEASURE
OF OUR SUCCESS

THE
MEASURE
OF OUR

AN IMPASSIONED PLEA TO PASTORS

SUCCESS

SHAWN LOVEJOY

BakerBooks

a division of Baker Publishing Group
Grand Rapids, Michigan

Published by Baker Books
a division of Baker Publishing Group
P.O. Box 6287, Grand Rapids, MI 49516-6287
www.bakerbooks.com

Printed in the United States of America

Library of Congress Cataloging-in-Publication Data
Lovejoy, Shawn, 1971–
    The measure of our success : an impassioned plea to pastors / Shawn
Lovejoy.
        p.   cm.
    Includes bibliographical references (p.   ).
    ISBN 978-0-8010-1460-4 (pbk.)
    1. Pastoral theology. 2. Success—Religious aspects—Christianity. I. Title.
BV4211.3.L68 2012
253—dc23   2012000561

12   13   14   15   16   17   18   7   6   5   4   3   2   1

In keeping with biblical principles of creation stewardship, Baker Publishing Group advocates the responsible use of our natural resources. As a member of the Green Press Initiative, our company uses recycled paper when possible. The text paper of this book is composed in part of post-consumer waste.

This work is dedicated first to my Lord;
then to my wife, Tricia, and my kids,
Hannah, Madison, and Paul—all of whom
have displayed great grace in my life.

CONTENTS

Contents

PART 1

STANDARD MEASUREMENTS

1

WHAT'S WRONG
WITH PASTORS?

Over the last few years, while serving as a pastor and leader of Churchplanters.com, I have been honored to consult, interact with, coach, and survey hundreds of pastors and ministry leaders across our nation. Today I am deeply convinced of one truth: pastors are not doing so well. Most pastors are disillusioned, discouraged, and discontent with the way their lives and ministries are turning out. Even in the church planting movement, which has seemed successful on the surface, many detect a "disturbance in the Force."

In my work as a pastor and with Churchplanters.com, I have learned about numerous heartbreaking situations. Just this past year three pastors I know personally have had extramarital affairs and lost their ministries. I am talking about long-term, secret relationships with people in their churches. All the while they were preaching every week and leading "explosive" ministries. Another pastor friend attempted suicide this past year. Yet another pastor was admitted to the hospital and placed on suicide watch after being forced to resign from his church after years of secret domestic abuse in his marriage. Events like these are happening in ministry circles all across America.

Pastors, whether or not we want to pretend, many of us are hurting. We are not experiencing the fruits of the Spirit, and we are not thriving relationally. I am sick and tired of pastors getting picked off by the enemy like this! Thus, this impassioned plea to pastors.

Recent research has backed up what for years I have sensed and seen. A study by my good friends Ed Stetzer of Lifeway Research and Todd Wilson of the Exponential Network has seemed to prove once again that most pastors are not experiencing success or feeling successful. In their recent research, most pastors admitted to struggling with

1. the battle to overcome pride, self-reliance, and drivenness;
2. loneliness and isolation;
3. mistrust;
4. lack of rest; and
5. maintaining a sense of joy.

"Although most church planters understand the importance of making personal development and family nurturing top priorities," the report stated, "these things often get lost in a planter's busyness."[1] This is yet another indicator that all is not well in ministry world.

Why am I writing this book? Because all this is breaking my heart. All this angers me to the core. All this could break my spirit. I love the local church. I love pastors. I believe in both. I believe God has so much he still wants to do in and through pastors committed to his church and his mission. However, it has become very obvious to me that for God to have his way in and through us, something has to radically change. Things have to improve. I want pastors to begin to thrive again. Pastors, I want us to win! I want the church to win! That is why I decided to write this impassioned plea to pastors.

The question I've been asking is very simple: Why? Why are so many pastors and ministry leaders falling? Why are they so vulnerable? Why are they so unfulfilled? Lonely? Insecure? Discouraged? Depressed? Burned out? Why are so many not seeing the fruit they hoped they would see? What is wrong with pastors? I have grappled with these questions for some time now. As I have counseled the many men and women who have dealt with the aftermath of unwise choices or struggled with burnout and fatigue, my goal has always been to do more than put a Band-Aid on the problem. I want to know how they got there so we can all avoid following the same path in the future. I want us

> **Our root problem is that we have exchanged God's definition of success for our own.**

to learn from our mistakes. How could someone so in love with Jesus reach the point of walking away, cashing it all in, or giving it all up? How could someone who looks so credible to a watching world be so broken and deceptive behind closed doors?

I have wrestled with this. I have prayed over this. I have talked with many ministry leaders who are winning, some who are losing, and many who are struggling. Here's my basic conclusion: the main reason so many of us are struggling stems from our definition of success. Somewhere along our ministry journey, we got things tangled up in our hearts and heads. Our root problem is that we have exchanged God's definition of success for our own. We have begun to measure success the way the world does. I call these assessments standard measurements.

Some of the standard measurements of success out there are contributing to this mess, and I want to address them in this work. I doubt any of them will totally surprise you. What's surprising is that, up until recently, I hadn't even heard pastors warning each other about them. We must talk about them. We must ask God to deliver us from these idols of standard measurement. We must ask God to teach us what real success is and rescue us from the destruction that ensues when we take our eyes off his measure of success. Where do we start? With our own motivations. This is my impassioned plea to pastors—for all of us to radically alter our measures of success.

THE DANGER OF DRIVENNESS

Ambitious. Self-starter. Entrepreneurial. Strong work ethic. Discontent with the status quo. Big vision. Change agent. Strong leader and communicator. Get-things-done type of person. Driven.

All of these describe me. The argument could even be made that these traits have contributed to our church's "success." For years I have held these personal traits up as a badge of honor. I have held these characteristics in high regard, and I have also wanted to surround myself with team members who are wired the same way. I am not the only one either. Referring to his team, one senior pastor told me, "I'd rather pull them back and make them take time off than have to kick them in the rear all the time." No senior pastor wants a lazy team member. That's fair, isn't it?

The church has so much work to do. Our mission is monumental, and our tasks are unending. Jesus told us to go. People need to be reached. People need to be saved! Ministries need to be launched and stewarded well. The details of ministry must be handled with excellence. Let's be honest, ministry is not a nine-to-five job, is it? Pastors and ministry leaders often must be willing to take their work home with them. I think pastors ought to be the hardest working people in the world, because our mission has so much on the line! Ambition and drive certainly seem to be critical success factors for pastors in growing ministries across America.

This is not at all bad. Not long ago, it seemed like pastors had more of a reputation for being lazy and overweight and working only one day a week! I think it's safe to say that we have now blown that myth to pieces. Most pastors I know are highly driven to be the best men, fathers, husbands, and pastors they can be. I rub elbows with a bunch of ambitious go-getters who feel called by God to change the world for Jesus Christ.

The question is, has the pendulum swung too far the other way? Let's be honest: as ambitious self-starters, we can so easily begin to work *for* Jesus at the expense of working *in and through* Jesus. The more talented and driven we are, the easier it becomes for us to rely on our own ambition, talents, power, strength, intellect, and wisdom. We probably have the best of intentions, but at times our drive to succeed overrides God's plans. Many times we unconsciously run ahead of him in our desire to be successful in carrying out the Great Commission. Haven't we all, at one time or another, gotten caught up in our own plans and realized that we have strayed from what God actually called us to do? Yet God has cautioned us: "Trust in the LORD with all your heart and lean not on your own understanding" (Prov. 3:5 NIV). I have told our church on many occasions that the greatest temptation I face is not stealing the money from the offering or having an affair; the greatest temptation I face is substituting what I do *for* God for what I am *with* God.

One of the great challenges I see with some of the most gifted men and women in the church is this: our greatest assets, when used outside of Christ's lordship, become our greatest liabilities. The same talents and personalities that make us great pastors become highly destructive outside the bounds of the Spirit's control. For instance, there's nothing wrong with our desire to work hard, to be the best, to strive for excellence, or even to be successful. However, that drive must be directed by the Holy Spirit to keep it from becoming selfish ambition. Paul, under God's inspiration, warned us about this: "Do *nothing* out of selfish ambition or vain conceit"

Our greatest assets, when used outside of Christ's lordship, become our greatest liabilities.

(Phil. 2:3 NIV, emphasis added). Being driven is a good thing until that drive overrides the drive of the Spirit.

Compounding the challenge at this point is the fact that we don't even understand our own motives! We don't even recognize what is driving us. We don't often understand why we do what we do. If we could really see what's in our hearts, I believe we would come to the conclusion that what's propelling us forward is often not the Holy Spirit—it's testosterone, or just plain old flesh.

As pastors, the greatest battle we face is not a battle against our ministries. It's the battle between our flesh and his Spirit. Why do we really care so much about how many showed up for church this past weekend? Why is one of the first questions we ask each other as pastors about the size of our churches? Why are the financial contribution numbers really so important? Are these things representative of our ability to make disciples, or more about making budget and paying the bills? Why do we care so much about baptism numbers? Why do we want to start a new site versus plant a new church? Why are we unwilling to plant churches in our own neighborhood? Why do we want to broadcast ourselves to as many places and screens as possible?

I believe that gut-level honest answers to many of these questions would often reveal that even though we preach against it, our ministries are often being driven by our flesh, not the Spirit. Paul said, "For those who live according to the flesh set their minds on the things of the flesh, but those who live according to the Spirit set their minds on the things of the Spirit" (Rom. 8:5 ESV). So what are those things of the flesh that tend to drive us?

AFFIRMATION

We all like to be affirmed. We all need to be affirmed. However, affirmation can also become an idol. It can become what we live for. We can live, preach, and lead with our only goal being the affirmation of others. I feel the same temptation as you to gauge my weekend success by the number of compliments I get on my sermon or the services. If I get tons of compliments, it was a good day; if not, it was not. I will say that I think this is one of the areas I win in more often than not. Affirmation is not necessarily my major love language. One of the reasons I think that's so is the fact that I felt so affirmed by my dad as a young man growing up. He loved me, affirmed me, encouraged me, believed in me, and has always been my biggest fan. I really think that my sense of self-worth and confidence is healthier because of my strong relationship with an affirming dad. Dads have that kind of power! However, a troubling trend in ministry is becoming evident with the disintegration of the healthy family in our country. Many pastors (if not most) have grown up with unhealthy, unstable relationships with their dads. One pastor told me that all his dad ever affirmed in his life was an A on his report card and his wins on the

> **As pastors, the greatest battle we face is not a battle against our ministries. It's the battle between our flesh and his Spirit.**

baseball field. The implication? Nothing less than the best and winning at all costs were good enough. He has struggled with being anything less than the best his whole life. Sometimes his drive to be noticed and affirmed has gotten him into trouble. That is just one scenario.

I personally believe that some of the struggles many other men, pastors included, have with both affirmation and authority stem from an unhealthy father-son relationship. I am no psychologist, but I have noticed a connection between an unhealthy drive, an unhealthy response to authority, and an unhealthy relationship with Dad. I'm not the only one who sees the connection either. One denominational executive who has administered many church planter assessments told me, "The father relationship piece has become so evident in our assessments that it has almost become a deal breaker for us. If a young man has not had a healthy relationship with Dad, we might not support them." Wow. Does an unhealthy relationship with Dad guarantee unhealthiness? No. Can we overcome an unhealthy relationship with our dad? Absolutely. I have seen it done. However, what we can't do is sweep our own baggage under the rug. We must confront and deal with the issues from our past that could cause us to be driven in unhealthy ways. If we don't, it will all catch up with us as it has caught up with many.

NUMBERS

So many pastors define themselves and their ministries by the numbers. Ask any pastor how he or she is doing, and this is usually the answer: "We're doing pretty well. We just had the largest Easter we've ever had. We're running about X in attendance. We've baptized X people this year. We've got X services now on X campuses. God is blessing!"

Now, I promise, as you will see in these pages, I have nothing against growth and numbers. My ministry team looks at numbers regularly. We run reports and graphs. We track attendance and baptisms. Numbers can be one measurement of health and even success, but numbers alone can be the most deceptive measure of success there is. I personally know of two pastors who were experiencing explosive numerical growth in their churches while they were committing adultery in their churches. To be clear, this is not success. That just reminds us that numbers do not tell the whole story. Numbers alone simply cannot be the measure of our success.

I must also confess something to you here and now: I have played the numbers game. I have allowed the attendance metric to inflate or deflate my self-esteem. We have made various lists of the "Top 100" churches a couple of times, and I must admit it felt *really* good. Since that time, however, I have become an anti-fan of these lists. All they do is tempt one hundred pastors to become more prideful and discourage tens of thousands of pastors who will never make the list. And if we're honest, we know we are all tempted to do everything we can, at the expense of every relationship we have, to get on these lists. However, these lists simply do not define success. Success is being faithful with what we have.

At times I have been guilty of measuring myself and my abilities against the attendance in my church and the attendance in the churches of others. I am still tempted to measure success by the numbers. I have even coached pastors and church planters to structure their churches for "launching large" and experiencing "exponential" growth and on how to "break growth barriers" and move on to "megachurch status."

However, I believe one of the reasons pastors are struggling is that they wake up one day only to realize that they will not be the next pastor whose church doubles in attendance every year. Those euphoric years, if ever achieved, are usually short-lived. Most churches, if growing numerically at all, grow 5 to 10 percent per year. Many of us are simply not okay with that picture. If our church isn't growing exponentially, we are not happy. Why? We don't feel successful.

My great friend and mentor Larry Osborne, one of the senior pastors of North Coast Church in San Diego, California, and author of *Sticky Church*, has been one of the men who has helped me to change my thought process. He has told me numerous times that North Coast's goal is to assimilate 80 percent of however many they grow by each year into their small group ministry. That's all. He told me their history indicated this was the maximum number of people they were able to assimilate into biblical community each year. To grow in attendance but not assimilate those people into a true community does not constitute a win for North Coast. That should be true for all of us. If our attendance growth comes at the expense of our ability to disciple people, we have not been successful.

As I write this, the community I serve at Mountain Lake Church is certainly not doubling in attendance every year. We could not be good stewards of that kind of growth. Do we measure stuff at our church? Of course we do. We are just careful not to measure by attendance alone. We measure the percentage of attendance we have active in biblical community. By "biblical community" we mean groups of people who are connecting *together* with God, doing life with and serving each other, and reaching out to people outside the community of believers. Biblical community is about much more than being assimilated or involved in a Bible study. For instance, I don't believe a closed group doing Bible study only can be considered biblical community. Such groups of people might be assimilated; we might be closing the back door by getting them connected. But they are not functioning as the body of Christ the way they should if they are not doing his mission. Our small groups are low control but high accountability in this regard. We must measure *biblical* community, not just community. The Elks Lodge, the Rotary Club, and Alcoholics Anonymous have community. The church simply must be more.

We currently have over 65 percent of our attendees active in volunteerism and ministry in our church. We have also maintained over 70 percent of our attendance active in small groups for most of our history. However, "assimilating people" can't be the only measure of our success. Assimilating people is not enough. We work diligently within our volunteer and small group structures to ensure that biblical community can grow. We measure how many of our small groups serve in our community each semester. Our groups are held accountable for "getting off the couch" and going out to serve people groups and families in our community, nation, and world. We measure the number of people we send around the world to minister. This year we will send out over four hundred people through our World Care ministry.

We measure the frequency with which our ministry team meets with their volunteer leaders each month, because we cannot disciple our leaders unless we spend time with them. We also don't just measure our financial giving; we measure our per capita giving (our giving per person). We have tracked this number over time. This number has grown by about one dollar per person per year every year since the church began. That means our church is becoming more generous over time. We are developing maturing disciples of Christ!

Notice something else about the measurements I've just mentioned: these percentages and ratios can be a picture of health no matter the size of the church. In other words, there is a way to measure success that has nothing to do with being large. We don't have to be large to be successful! Our call is to make disciples. Jesus didn't say, "Go and grow large." He said, "Go and make disciples" (Matt. 28:19 NIV). I am more convinced than ever before that most churches are not supposed to be large. The more we try to make ourselves so, the more stressed and discouraged we're going to become. Are you getting the picture?

> **Jesus didn't say, "Go and grow large." He said, "Go and make disciples" (Matt. 28:19 NIV).**

I must confess that at times I have forgotten that success cannot always be measured by numbers. In the Gospels, Jesus and the apostles measured success by stories more than by numbers.

I must confess I still get that backward sometimes. In doing so I place a yoke on myself that Jesus never placed on me. I have sought to grow our church bigger and faster than perhaps what Jesus was even asking of me. Because of this tendency, I have at times placed an unfair burden on myself and, through our influence, other pastors as well. For that I have repented to God. I repent to you today as well. God has forgiven me; he will forgive you and make your burden lighter again too, if you will take his yoke over the one anyone else might try to put on you!

ACTIVITY

Another common measurement of our success is activity. Churches are busy—and proud of it, aren't we? We love to boast about all we're doing on the Web and in our worship guides. We advertise in our communities and in local papers about all the ministries we offer. One church in our area has billboards all over the community that boast of "over 152 ministries for you and your family." We all seek to provide activities for every age range on almost every day of the week. Pastors drive more of that than we want to take credit (or blame) for. Don't get me wrong; I think pastors ought to be busy. Jesus himself said, "I must be about My Father's business" (Luke 2:49 NKJV). However, most pastors are too busy.

We are constantly looking for the next program, activity, or study that's going to help us make disciples. I'll talk more about discipleship later. However, if my conversations with ministry leaders have taught me anything, it's this: busyness does not equal effectiveness. It's often actually a distraction. Many pastors stay busy because we feel like busyness is discipleship. Many of us have believed the lie that says busyness is value. We love to feel needed. We love being problem solvers and crisis counselors. We feel important when the phone rings a lot and we have a lot to do. We unconsciously enjoy telling people, even other pastors, how busy we are. We wear our busyness as a badge of honor. If we were honest, we'd admit that much of our activity is driven by the desire to be needed. In the end, though, I think most of us know deep down that activity does not equal success.

APPROVAL

Closely related to our desire to be needed as pastors is our need for approval. Approval is another common measure of success. We want people to approve of our actions, our methods, our style, and our decisions. Many of us are driven by our desire to be liked or affirmed. Who doesn't want to be liked? However, if not held in check, that desire can lead to dark places.

I've seen the limitations this unchecked desire can place on a young leader time and again. Someone who is brought up in a dysfunctional family, in which affirmation and love do not abound, is more likely to seek approval from other people than is someone who felt secure love, acceptance, and affirmation from his or her parents. A lack of affirmation can cause a young leader to feel he or she always has something to prove. I've seen these men and women driven by forces they don't even understand, and I believe much of it can be traced back to a desire for approval. Although they desire to please God, many of them still harbor a deep need to be liked and accepted by people, above all else, and that can radically affect their decision making, conflict management, and overall leadership.

Scripture reminds us all, however, that we must be careful not to let our motivation for ministry come from a desire to be people pleasers. This is not a new temptation. Paul wrestled with this very thing. Thank God he defeated that temptation: "Obviously, I'm not trying to win the approval of people, but of God. If pleasing people were my goal, I would not be Christ's servant" (Gal. 1:10). Approval from others cannot be the measure of our success!

FAME

Closely related to approval, flat-out fame can become another measure of success. Now, no pastor would ever admit to getting into the ministry to be famous. Our hearts are deceitful, though, aren't they? Sometimes I think our desire for "growth" and "influence" is just an unconscious desire to be noticed. Too many of us are more concerned about what other pastors think about our ministries than about what people in our own churches think about our character. Most of us care far too much about the number of Facebook friends, blog readers, and Twitter followers we have. We keep a secret eye on how many times our wisdom is retweeted, and we feel validated and important if we can write an article, speak at a conference, or gain a voice in a larger forum.

Pastors, are we trying to get people to follow us or follow Jesus? The church has too many pastor-followers as it is, and I believe it has become a detriment to the health of the body of Christ. We might just change the world if we would stop worrying about 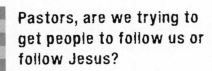 **Pastors, are we trying to get people to follow us or follow Jesus?** how many people are following us and instead start helping people follow Jesus in our own churches.

The truth is, everyone looks more glamorous from a distance. We all look dirtier up close. I know many famous pastors, and they're not nearly as perfect as they seem from a distance. Trust me, I'm not either. Before I decided to write this book, I had to ask myself, "Why do I want to write this? What do I really hope to achieve?" I must strive every day to keep my motivations in check, because "pride goes before destruction, and haughtiness before a fall" (Prov. 16:18). Fame simply cannot be the measure of a pastor's success.

Numbers. Activity. Approval. Fame. All of us are tempted to measure our success by these standards. These are all things that can drive our lives and our ministries and, if they do, result in some devastating moral or emotional fallout. These standards aren't just wrong measurements; they are idols of the heart. They are the very roots of sin and idol worship in our lives. We who lead and model the way must repent. Daily. We of all people must tear down the idols in our hearts and lives. We need to find a new standard of measurement. We must live for an audience of one. I am with you on the journey. I know these idols well, because these are the same idols that creep into my life and heart continually. On this journey, we will repent together. We will get honest with God and each other, and we will ask God to help us rediscover his measure of success.

INSIGHT

Larry Osborne, author and pastor
of North Coast Church, Vista, CA

My mentor warned me: most pastors are basically inse-cure. I think he might have been a little tough on pastors. The truth is, most people are insecure.

Having said that, insecurity in the heart of a pastor is an especially dangerous thing. It leads to priorities, decisions, and actions that are more about lifting up the pastor than lifting up Jesus.

We may know intellectually that faithfulness isn't mea-sured by the size of our church, that it's foolish to compare ourselves with others, and that a bigger church isn't nec-essarily a healthier church. But when insecurity reigns, all that goes out the window.

That's why I'm so grateful that one of my early mentors never stopped pounding into my head his favorite ministry motto: "We have nothing to prove and no one to impress."

The first time I heard him say it, I knew he was right. I also sensed that it would change everything if I could ever get to the point that I genuinely believed it and lived by it.

It took a while, but finally it clicked for me at the end of my third year as the pastor of North Coast Church. Those were tough years. Not much went right. Along with near zero growth, we had a constant undercurrent of conflict. It was a season of significant depression. My wife and I still call it "the dark years."

Then suddenly, everything changed. The sun shined. But not for the reasons you might think. Our ministry didn't suddenly turn around. We didn't experience a massive growth spurt. Instead, God gave me a spiritual kick in the gut.

I can't even remember the exact event. I'm not sure I even knew I was wrestling with God. All I remember is a sudden and intense awareness that he was not pleased with my value system and the way I was evaluating my lack of "ministry success."

He showed me that the thought process that was leading to my depression (*Our church isn't growing; it's all my fault; I must be a bad person and pastor*) was identical to the thought process that produces arrogance when things go well (*Our church is growing; it's all my doing; God is lucky to have me on his side*).

It shook me to the core. My insecurity and depression were nothing more than the mirror images of arrogance and haughtiness. The only difference was that one flowed out of my failures and one flowed out of my successes.

That day I began a complete realignment of my ministry scorecard. I found I really could find my identity in Christ, not the size of my church. I began to rediscover the joy that flows out of the *privilege* of ministry rather than the *successes* of ministry.

Best of all, I found myself inching a little closer toward a life and ministry aligned with the motto of my mentor: nothing to prove, no one to impress—except Jesus.

QUESTIONS FOR MEASUREMENT

1. Of the standard measurements listed in the chapter, which one tempts you the most? Why?

2. What do you enjoy most in ministry: crowds, small groups, or one-on-one encounters?

3. If you were telling Jesus your answers to the first two questions, would he agree with you?

4. What would it look like for your church to measure more by the story than by the number? How could you express this shift in your church?

2

THE THREE Cs OF UNHEALTHY MEASUREMENT

WHAT SHOULDN'T COUNT BUT DOES

Before I entered vocational ministry, I worked in the real estate profession. Actually, I was in the middle of taking over the very successful family real estate business in my hometown. As a twenty-two-year-old kid, I was pulling down a six-figure income, surrounded by friends and family, and making a name for myself. My future could not have been brighter. Suffice it to say, I was a self-assured, confident young man. Maybe even a little cocky.

Then God called me into vocational ministry. My confidence buoyed any reservations I might have felt. Sure, I knew the change in careers meant major lifestyle adjustments, but I was sure that I was more than able to conquer the world for Jesus.

My confidence was a driving force in my life—that is, until I entered vocational ministry. As I encountered the challenges of ministry, I began to understand that not everyone was going to like me. Not everyone was going to come to my church. Not everyone was going to stay at my church. I experienced the underbelly of ministry, complete with its relational conflict, squandered resources, and lack of leadership support. I still expressed confidence on the outside, but I was scared to death on the inside. Could I really be effective? Did my ideas have merit? Could I demonstrate effective leadership? Could I manage a staff? Would I actually make a difference? I had never doubted myself so much as when I entered vocational ministry. Then I started a church: talk about self-doubt!

I had never doubted myself so much as when I entered vocational ministry.

Can you relate to that? There's just something about the weight of vocational ministry that causes us to doubt who we are and how God made us. We feel the burden of doing our best for the one who called us. But somewhere in there, we get tangled up in staffing or church conflict or circumstances that are far above our pay grade. Sometimes we make the right call. Sometimes we don't. To put it simply, Satan is out to get us. Scripture paints a clear picture of our enemy's desire to wreak havoc on God's plan and purposes. If Satan can cause us to feel insecure about our own leadership and calling, he's got us headed down a slippery slope to ineffectiveness, insecurity, discouragement, and defeat.

As a pastor or ministry leader, you've probably studied, or at least read about, the three Cs of hiring: chemistry, competence, and character. The idea behind the three Cs is that it's dangerous to hire anyone who doesn't rate highly in all three areas. However, you've probably never heard of what I call the three Cs of unhealthy measurement: comparing, copying, and condemning. These three Cs can cripple our potential and stagnate growth. Ultimately, they reveal themselves when we are not physically, emotionally, or spiritually healthy. Without realizing the damage that can be done, we are often driven by one or more of these three Cs of unhealthy measurement that find their basis in insecurity. I'm convinced that much of what drives us in our ministries is our own insecurity as we seek to measure ourselves and our ministries against our own comrades in the faith.

Maybe that's why Paul said what he did to his young mentee, Timothy: "As for you, always be sober-minded, endure suffering, do the work of an evangelist, fulfill *your* ministry" (2 Tim. 4:5 ESV, emphasis added).

After studying this passage of Scripture in six different translations and in the original language, do you know what I discovered? I could not find one translation that reads, "fulfill Rick Warren's ministry," or "fulfill Mark Driscoll's ministry," or "fulfill T. D. Jakes's ministry." I didn't even find "fulfill the ministry of X Community Church." Can you believe that? The apostle Paul, under the inspiration of the Holy Spirit, actually said, "Fulfill *your* ministry."

An amazing sense of freedom comes with becoming secure in our own skin, secure in who we are, and secure in what God has called us to be and do. Do you remember what Jesus said? "Come to me, all you who are weary and burdened, and I will give you rest. Take my yoke upon you and learn from me, for I am gentle and humble in heart, and you will find rest for your souls. For my

> **An amazing sense of freedom comes with becoming secure in our own skin, secure in who we are, and secure in what God has called us to be and do.**

yoke is easy and my burden is light" (Matt. 11:28–30 NIV). He assures us that a distinctive sense of rest and peace will come into our lives and ministries when we take off the burdens that we place on ourselves or allow others to place on us (including those placed on us by well-meaning religious leaders) and we replace them with the mission that Jesus has uniquely designed for us.

Here's the challenge: If we begin to measure ourselves in an unhealthy way; if we doubt who we are and the abilities God has given us; and if we we allow yokes to be placed on us that Jesus did not intend, an insatiable desire to be like someone else will creep in. If we become insecure in our own calling, we will measure ourselves by the success of others.

COMPARING

Two years after launching Mountain Lake, we were running approximately two hundred attendees. Twitter and Facebook did not exist, and blogs had not yet become the way we kept up with the world. Without these outside sources of social media, I had a very narrow view of success. I thought Mountain Lake was the fastest-growing church in the world! We felt like the kings of the world! My team felt like they were leading a movement! Those were the days when breaking the "two hundred barrier" within two years as a church plant was a remarkable achievement. That's certainly not the case anymore, at least it's implied.

Because of the technology available today, we can always find a church that's building it bigger, better, and faster than we are! We read the status updates and the blog posts, and suddenly, what is happening at our church is not good enough. We realize our creativity is anything but. Our growth is not quite as impressive. Our facilities are lacking. We aren't staffed as well. We're not baptizing as many people as' *they* are. Simply put, our church pales in comparison!

COPYING

So what do we do? Well, when our church is not growing as quickly as another, we begin to think, "Maybe if our church was more like their church, we would be growing faster." That's when we begin copying another successful leader's strategy or tactics, hoping to reproduce what God has done in that ministry. We surf the Web. We take a few notes. We tweak our vision or rip off theirs altogether. We begin viewing, listening, and downloading. Now we're doing the same message series, singing the same songs, and using the same language on our church website, in the blogosphere, and on social networks. We decide to attend their conference. We even notice their attire and make a mental note. Have you been to a "successful" pastors' conference lately? We even all dress the same!

Don't get me wrong. I'm a raving advocate for sharing resources and ideas. I have learned much about church and preaching from other churches. I have ripped off innovative ideas from other pastors. I also share sermon ideas and creative elements with the pastors I coach and the churches we plant. And yes, I confess to a passion for knock-off designer jeans and cool shoes. What I'm speaking to goes more to the heart of the leader. Methods can be shared; confidence in our calling cannot.

When comparing ourselves to and copying other pastors doesn't produce the growth in our ministry that it has in theirs, we get discouraged. We're tempted to believe that God isn't blessing us or that he has forgotten us. We might even become bitter, since this whole ministry thing isn't quite turning out the way we dreamed it would. Often our first instinct is not to look inward. We choose to look outward.

CONDEMNING

We begin the Christian version of trash talk. We begin to condemn other leaders and their ministries. We think to ourselves, "Well, if their ministry is growing at that rate, they must be watering down the Word." (One of the funniest tweets I've ever read came from my friend Tony Morgan, who once tweeted:

"I'm in a jammed and crowded Mexican restaurant. I wonder if anyone will accuse them of watering down the salsa.") We might even catch ourselves saying negative things about other pastors whose churches are bigger than ours or too close to ours. We question motives, intentions, and methods. And don't think those questions are based on some noble righteousness. Often our jealousy is driving us, not our zeal for godly leadership. What are we doing? Aren't we all on the same team? Wouldn't we—and the world—benefit from our unity rather than our division? Too many of us are condemning other leaders simply because we're insecure in our own skin. Jealousy breeds condemnation.

> Too many of us are condemning other leaders simply because we're insecure in our own skin. Jealousy breeds condemnation.

In the final stage of this vicious cycle, when condemning what everyone else is doing doesn't make us feel any better, we finally take a hard look at ourselves. A condemning look. We think maybe the best thing for us to do is just get out of the way, step down, find a way out, quit, escape, and move to the next big thing in the next city that might produce the measure of success we so deeply desire. The grass is always greener on the other church campus, isn't it? Sound familiar? The most depressing element in all of this is the fact that without a true change of heart, we'll repeat this vicious cycle over and over again.

All three of the dangerous Cs—comparing, copying, and condemning—are symptoms of the larger problem many pastors face: they are not measuring themselves or their ministries the way God does. Too many of us are trying to fulfill someone else's ministry. Because of this there are too many cookie-cutter pastors, churches, and ministries and not enough pastors fulfilling their unique callings.

DRESSING FOR SUCCESS

We're not the first spiritual leaders ever to struggle with insecurity, fear, and the temptation to run when life's battles seem bigger than we are. King David, the man after God's own heart, is a great example of someone who was tempted to be insecure in his own skin:

> Then Saul gave David his own armor—a bronze helmet and a coat of mail. David put it on, strapped the sword over it, and took a step or two to see what it was like, for he had never worn such things before.
> "I can't go in these," he protested to Saul. "I'm not used to them." So David took them off again. He picked up five smooth stones from a stream and put them into his shepherd's bag. Then, armed only with his shepherd's staff and sling, he started across the valley to fight the Philistine. (1 Sam. 17:38–40)

On this day, David had a choice: try to fight this huge battle like someone else had done it, using someone else's tools and weapons, or fight the battle in his own unique way—the way God had given him. I think David is a remarkable example for us in regard to our modern-day insecurities. Just as David had to decide how he would dress for battle, so must we, and many of us are trying to fight the battles of ministry dressed like someone else! We're trying to wear someone else's armor.

Someone else's armor might be someone else's personality. Saul was a great soldier who had won many battles. David, however, was not a soldier. He was an ordinary shepherd, and he knew that to have any chance to win the battle, he couldn't fight like a soldier. He needed to fight like a shepherd. That was who he was. You and I are in the same predicament. If we want to win the ministry battles God has ahead for us, we need to fight them with the tools God has given us. We need to stop trying to preach like, lead like, or, God forbid, dress like someone else!

Someone else's armor could be someone else's talent or skill. Many pastors preach the parable of the talents, but most of us never apply it to our lives and ministries. Let me tell you a secret: most of us will never teach like Andy Stanley, Matt Chandler, or Tony Evans. Most of us will never lead like Bill Hybels or Rick Warren. And the best part is that we're not supposed to!

Let me give you some perspective. Did you know that there are only 1,400 megachurches in America right now? Did you know that this number has not grown in over a decade? Most new churches are not growing to megachurch status. Odds are that most of us will never pastor a megachurch, and we are not supposed to! God gave us a certain amount of talent, and he only holds us accountable for the gifts we have. Success is not reaching megachurch status. Success is using the skills and talents God gave each of us to live out the mission he assigned to us.

I know what it's like to hear a voice in your head telling you that if you were more like Pastor X or your church were more like Church X across town, you could be more "successful." However, I am here to tell you, that voice is from the evil one! How do I know that? I have listened to that voice, and it has always led me to dark places. Today I am learning to listen to that still small voice that says, "Shawn, you don't need to wear someone

> **Are we willing to take off all the artificial stuff we've been trying to wear and start being who we were meant to be?**

else's armor to win." I'm actually finding that the more I lean into the personality and gifts God has given me, the more successful my ministry becomes. I can also feel my sense of freedom, significance, and self-worth return to normal!

Here's a question to ponder: What do you think would have happened if David had tried to fight the battle with someone else's armor—armor that didn't fit his size or skill set? His movement would have been limited, for sure, and it probably would have gotten him killed. Could it be that you and I are limiting the movement of God in our churches because we're trying to fight the battle in someone else's armor? Could it be that we relentlessly pursue church growth—numbers, activity, approval, or fame—because we are insecure in our own skin and in our own armor? Could our anxiety, fatigue, and discouragement be symptoms of "success syndrome"? The question I believe God is asking us today is this: Are we willing to take off all the artificial stuff we've been trying to wear and start being who we were meant to be?

INSIGHT

Steven Furtick, author of Sun Stand Still *and lead pastor of Elevation Church, Charlotte, NC*

Pastor Shawn has done an incredible job outlining an issue that many pastors face: How do I stay faithful to who God has called me to be? This is a real challenge because you can always find somebody doing what you're trying to do better than you're doing it. If you're not careful, you'll fall into the trap of the three Cs that Pastor Shawn has so accurately described: comparing, copying, and condemning.

The truth is, God has no set paradigm for how he works through us. He wants to do new things in new places at new times with new people. And the strategy that God used to work a miracle in one setting might actually cause a church split in yours.

By all means, study other great leaders' best practices. But don't make the mistake of thinking that one of their systems can create a move of God. You can't build a God-infused ministry by trying to mimic the miracles that God has already worked through other people. Leaders are first and foremost models of faith before they are models of ministry. So when you study what God is doing through other great leaders, make sure you look most closely at their faith.

I love how Pastor Shawn uses the story of Saul giving his armor to David in 1 Samuel 17. It didn't fit David—he was a shepherd boy, and Saul was a great warrior and a king. I love David's response in verses 39 and 40: he gave Saul his armor back, then went and got his little sling and some rocks.

David must have looked undignified, outdated, and beyond silly. But he stayed true to his skills and anointing. He played to his strengths and would not compromise who God had made him to be.

That's the key—don't try to mimic anybody else's miracle. Instead, imitate their faith in a God who can do the miraculous.

God wants to do powerful things through you that the world has never seen before. But he wants to do them through the bold faith that he has used and rewarded time and time again.

Listen to what Pastor Shawn is saying in this chapter. He's right on. You will never do Andy Stanley better than Andy, but you're the best you that God ever created!

QUESTIONS FOR MEASUREMENT

1. What does it mean to be tempted to wear someone else's armor?

2. Of the three Cs mentioned in the chapter, how are you most tempted to wear someone else's armor?

3. As best you know, what are you good at? What are your strengths? This is your armor! How could you lean into your unique strengths more often?

3

HOW DO THE MIGHTY FALL?

LIKE I DID

In the early days of starting Mountain Lake Church, I allowed the whole endeavor to bury me: emotionally, relationally, spiritually, and even physically. When I moved to metro Atlanta to start the church, my confidence was at an all-time high. I felt that I had sufficiently learned what to do and what not to do in leadership and ministry. Now, at the age of twenty-eight, I was planting a church. During my church planting assessment for a denominational agency, I actually had one church planting strategist ask me, "Well, you're just a little bit cocky, aren't you, Shawn?" A confident swagger? Yes. Maybe a little arrogance. But church planting has a way of humbling a guy. (Can I get a witness?)

The first two years at Mountain Lake were nothing explosive as far as growth is concerned. There were great moments, to be sure. Our grand opening was a day I'll never forget, with masses of people swirling around. Okay, 185 people, but that was a mass to me. Leading people into a relationship with Jesus, watching him restore broken lives, and helping others change the way they thought about church—all of it was exactly what I wanted. I absolutely wanted to be right in the middle of whatever God was doing.

We saw some miracles happen those first two years, but make no mistake: they were the two most difficult years of my life and ministry. So much demanded my attention. Although we had secured enough financial resources to support the church for two years, I was more aware than anyone of the deadline to be self-supporting. Church planters bear a unique double burden: win souls and establish financial partners. Without an influx of resources, our church certainly couldn't stay afloat. I always had one eye on the hearts of our people and one eye on our financial ability to open the doors next week.

> **I always had one eye on the hearts of our people and one eye on our financial ability to open the doors next week.**

Finances weren't my only concern. Marketing was another. We were new to the community, and we needed to meet people. I joined civic organizations to build relationships with the business community, and my wife joined a social group for stay-at-home moms. We also went totally old school and canvassed neighborhoods to invite people to Mountain Lake. We personally knocked on over one thousand doors. We spent evenings and weekends relentlessly investing in our community, leaving little time for each other.

Still, if my only concerns were financial and marketing, I might have thought church planting was a breeze. But I had never been a lead pastor before, which meant I had never preached on a weekly basis. Sermon prep was, and is, well . . . draining!

I didn't (and I still don't) take this part of my ministry lightly. Speaking on behalf of God weighed on me, and learning to craft messages that spoke to the masses, challenged them to change, and gave them the resources they needed to make a change was a skill I had to learn. I wasn't a preaching machine like so many of my peers. Although God had gifted me to be a communicator, I knew I had tons to learn.

As the founder and lead pastor, I was the buck-stops-here guy. I determined the culture, work ethic, and quality of my staff, and I was on a steep learning curve. Learning to walk the fine line between friendship and leadership wasn't something I enjoyed either. My heart and mind were always in overdrive with concerns for the men and women on my team as I balanced a desire to care for their needs and a demand to push them toward excellence.

I was exhausted. For two years, I thought of almost nothing besides Mountain Lake Church. It was an upstart, and it required constant attention. My wife and I understood at the forefront that our endeavor would require every ounce of our energy and determination, and it did. God never left my side, and he faithfully gave me words to speak. He used our team, and he taught me lessons I'm still benefiting from today, but I began to feel increasingly emotionally depleted from riding the roller coaster of financial uncertainty. Relationally, I also became tapped out. Physically, well, even though I had been an athlete and loved exercise, I hadn't worked out or taken care of myself at all. It was beginning to show. I wanted to serve God, but I wondered if I was measuring up. I wondered if he was going to use us to do something unique. I wondered if I would be successful.

Finally, two years into our new church, significant growth began to happen. Our church moved to a new location and doubled in size within a few weeks. *Doubled in size!* Our hard work, legwork, and diligence were beginning to pay off. Regular tithes and offerings had finally reached the point of making us a self-supported church, and although we weren't out of the woods financially, things were looking up. We even had enough to hire an additional staff member or two. As for me, I was already planning how to break through the next growth barrier.

For the first time in quite a while, I began to feel good about myself again. So good, in fact, that one night as my wife, Tricia, and I were lying in bed, I asked her, "Well, Trish, how do you think things are going?" Have you ever asked someone something but didn't really want to know the answer? I was actually just fishing for compliments. What I expected my wife to say was something like, "Wow, Shawn, things are going great. You are the greatest pastor and leader I've ever seen!" Instead, while staring at the bedroom ceiling, she answered my question with a question of her own: "Do you really want to know how I feel?"

I knew I was in trouble. If we will ask our spouses, "How do you think things are going?" and then shut up, they *will* tell us. Tricia began, "I don't think things are going well at all. I actually think you have allowed this church to turn you into a workaholic. You're never home. You never take a day off. I'm not even sure Hannah [our then two-year-old] knows you." She continued, "When you *are* home, you're always tired. You have a short fuse, and you're not all that fun to be around. In fact, there's a growing part of me wishing I had the Shawn who was up on the stage every week, humorous and happy, not the one who comes home with us. I'm not sure I like the person you've become."

She went on to say, "You never laugh any more at home. When I first met you in college, you were a cutup. You were always the life of the party. I loved your laugh. You made me laugh. But you never laugh anymore. We never laugh anymore." She didn't speak in anger or bitterness. As we lay in the dark that night, she spoke out of a broken heart. Maybe in the cover of darkness, where she couldn't see my response, she felt a little more secure sharing her true feelings.

Now, normally when my wife would try to play the role of the Holy Spirit in my life, I would instantly become defensive. This time, however, something miraculous happened. It was as if scales fell off my eyes immediately. I had been blind to it before, but now it was as if I could clearly see who I had become. Two years as a senior pastor and church planter, with all its unique burdens, had completely stolen my sense of joy. And as the spiritual leader of my family, I was robbing them of joy. I had not seen it, but my wife was right. Everything she had said about me was true. I recognized for the first time that night how spiritually, emotionally, physically, and relationally empty my life had become. Immediately I began to weep and repented to my wife and then to God. Tricia and I lay in bed and cried and prayed together. She continued to open up and share tons of pain that had accumulated in her heart over the last few years, and it wasn't easy to hear.

The next morning when we got up, I called my ministry partner and told him my wife and I needed to get away for a week. (We had not taken a vacation in three years.) I canceled everything on my calendar and left town with my family. Over the next seven days, Tricia and I took walks on the beach while we shouted at each other, cried with each other, prayed with each other, and shared pain with each other.

Near the end of the week, we began to turn a corner. We mapped out a plan to redeem our lives, our marriage, our family, and our ministry. We put boundaries in place to limit work time and make our home a soft place to fall again. I believe that week saved my marriage. I don't think Tricia ever would have actually left me. She always tells me she's in it for the long haul, so we would probably still be married. But I think our intimacy and friendship would have been sacrificed. So many people simply coexist in marriage, and I've never wanted that to be us. It would have been, though, if not for that week at the beach, if not for my wife speaking the truth in love to me.

Don't be fooled into thinking that your marriage is only between you and your spouse. It's not. If you are a spiritual leader, people look to you to be an example in every way, including in marriage. It's not private. It's a public testimony. My wife coaches other pastors' wives with this challenge: "If your marriage falters, what happens to your church? Your marriage is bigger than you and your husband. Do whatever it takes to keep your marriage healthy and strong so the people in your church can follow your lead." That's wisdom.

I believe that week saved my ministry too. I was headed for burnout or, even worse, derailment. I believe I would have quit or disqualified myself from the ministry eventually. Without a God-defined sense of success, I would have continued to deplete myself in every way. Thankfully, God preempted all of that.

Now, a decade after that tumultuous week at the beach, I can say that my marriage is healthy, strong, vibrant, and full of friendship, intimacy, and fun. Tricia and I have kept the promises we made to God and to each other during those long beach walks, and our boundaries are still intact today. It has not been easy. We have had to fight for health and intimacy. We still do. Life often gets in the way. In the pages to follow, I'll share with you how God and my spouse have fought for my spiritual,

> **Don't be fooled into thinking that your marriage is only between you and your spouse.**

emotional, relational, intellectual, and even physical health. At Churchplanters.com, a ministry geared toward helping pastors not only plant healthy churches but *be* healthy, we've come to call it "nurturing vitality." I'll tell you in the pages that follow how all of us can rediscover God's measure of success.

INSIGHT

J. D. Greear, lead pastor of Summit Church,
Raleigh-Durham, NC

One of most humbling yet liberating lessons I've learned as a pastor is that *God doesn't really need me*. When God spoke the world into existence, I wasn't around, and he didn't consult with me. Things have not changed for him. He is just as sufficient to do his work as he was the day he spoke it all into existence.

Jesus seemed to be constantly drilling this truth into his disciples. After giving them the Great Commission, he told them to do nothing until he sent "power from on High" (Luke 24:49; see Acts 1:4). I'm sure a few of the apostles were type A overachievers, and I can just hear one saying, "Wait! But there are people to win! Books to write! Conferences to plan! We've got to get to it—every second counts!" Yet he made them wait. If nothing else, Jesus was drilling into them that God didn't need them. This was a task he would do *through* them, not something they would do *for* him. He would build his church *using* them, but he did not depend on them. As they had seen, he could do more in ten minutes with five loaves and two fish than they could do in a year.

Shawn's transparency in this chapter helps us see that when we forget this truth and we take upon ourselves the role of God, we self-destruct. It's not that God doesn't want us to work hard. He does. But he wants us to do so as dependent servants, not as if we were him. At the end of the day, what God wants is faithfulness—first of all to him. This means fulfilling my responsibilities to my wife and family and taking care of myself. What I have to offer the church, I place into his hands. There's always more that could be done—five loaves and two fish are a meager offering in light of how big the crowd is. But he multiplies and uses it far beyond what I could ask or imagine.

God doesn't need you. Serve him because you love him and because you want to pour out your life in response to him, but not because he is in heaven wringing his hands with worry about whether you have what it takes. You don't. He does. Your responsibility is to be faithful, not to be God.

Perhaps the psalmist David captured it best. Through him God says,

> "If I were hungry, I would not tell you,
>   for the world and its fullness are mine.
> Do I eat the flesh of bulls
>   or drink the blood of goats?
> Offer to God a sacrifice of thanksgiving,
>   and perform your vows to the Most High,
> and call upon me in the day of trouble;
>   I will deliver you, and you shall glorify
>   me." (Ps. 50:12–15 ESV)

We glorify God by being faithful to him (v. 14) and by boldly asking him to bless our meager efforts beyond our wildest imaginations (v. 15).

For more on this, reflect on 2 Samuel 7:1–29; Psalm 46:10–11; Isaiah 44:24–28; John 6:1–14; 1 Corinthians 4:2; Ephesians 3:20–21; and Colossians 1:29.

QUESTIONS FOR MEASUREMENT

1. What part of Shawn's personal story impacted you the most?

2. Would you be willing to ask your spouse right now, "How do you think things are going?" Why or why not?

3. If you were to ask your spouse this question, how do you think they would answer?

PART 2

REDEFINING SUCCESS

4

NURTURING VITALITY

GETTING AND STAYING HEALTHY

I have good news: I am not going to advocate living a life of "balance." Balance means giving equal energy, focus, and attention to everything and everyone all the time. Sounds good, but I've never achieved it. On Easter Sundays, I have never been capable of giving equal time to the multiple worship services at church and the traditional family celebrations. Can't do it at Christmas either. During specific weeks and months of the year, various ministry engagements and activities drain all of my creative and relational energy, and I want to cocoon when I get home, not go for walks or play games with family or friends. On the flip side, when I'm enjoying a great meal with my wife, my mind isn't working out the details of an upcoming message series, and when my family is hiking in the North Georgia mountains, I'm much less aware of the needs of the people of my church. If I'm sitting at an Alabama football game, I may not even think about the fact that Mountain Lake Church exists. Consequently, my energy and attention are not balanced. I don't believe balance is possible. I don't even believe balance is biblical. Jesus's life certainly wasn't balanced. He worked mostly twelve-hour days, and he never had a full weekend off, as far as we know. Yet he still experienced a good family life and invested in his friendships. Based on the stories of his life and ministry found in Scripture, though, Jesus didn't live by the mantra of "God first, family second, ministry third." Once when Jesus was teaching, his mother and brother asked to speak with him, but he continued to teach the crowd (see Matt. 12:46). He didn't put his family first all the time.

So how did Jesus sustain the pace and handle the pressure while maintaining healthy relationships? As always, the answer is found in Scripture. "Very early in the morning, while it was still dark, Jesus got up, left the house and went off to a solitary place, where he prayed. Simon and his companions went to look for him, and when they found him, they exclaimed: 'Everyone is looking for you!' " (Mark 1:35–37 NIV).

The good news for us is that Jesus's life was undeniably unbalanced. He had to get up before daylight just to be alone. When crowds weren't surrounding him, he was either training the Twelve or healing a hurt. Early mornings and late nights characterized his ministry. Jesus indicated that sleep itself was even a challenge because of the nature of his call: "Foxes have dens and birds have nests, but the Son of Man has no place to lay his head" (Luke 9:58 NIV).

Everyone clamored for his attention—skeptics and believers alike—and he consistently made himself available to them, but he didn't work or serve at the discretion of the people. In other words, he wasn't available *all* the time. Strategically, Jesus pulled away from the crowds to rest and rejuvenate. Mark records the example of Jesus slipping away in the early morning hours to connect with his heavenly Father. Later, in Mark 6, we see that Jesus chose to nurture his vitality: "Then Jesus said, 'Let's go off by ourselves to a quiet place and rest awhile.' He said this because there were so many people coming and going that Jesus and his apostles didn't even have time to eat" (v. 31).

Doesn't sound balanced, does it? A balanced life and ministry certainly would have provided enough time to scarf down a sandwich or something, wouldn't it? In theory, yes, but not in rubber-meets-the-road life. Just like Jesus, all of us experience days—even seasons—when deadlines, demands, or burdens require all of our attention and even our energy. That's not a bad thing. Work is good. Ministry is a

> **How can we expect others to listen to our instruction if we don't even fully pattern our lives after Jesus?**

high calling worth every effort, and if we serve, we ought to do it with enthusiasm. Jesus modeled the way for us in this area. After an intense day or season, Jesus would pull away from the crowds and get his strength back again. He would hang out for a few days with Mary, Martha, Lazarus, and the disciples. He leveraged every minute he could for the kingdom, but he also "nurtured" his own vitality.

NURTURE VITALITY

To "nurture" is to feed, to nourish, to care for. To possess "vitality" is to possess strength, vibrancy, and health. We pastors need to care for, pay attention to, and be diligent about our own personal vibrancy and health as spiritual leaders. How can we effectively lead if we are falling apart on the inside? How can we expect others to listen to our instruction if we don't even fully pattern our lives after Jesus? Maybe a better question is, how long will the world give us credibility if we continue to fall and fail in church leadership? We must turn the tide and learn to follow the example Jesus set for us. Learning to renew and rejuvenate—to pull away from the crowds to rest awhile—just might be our saving grace.

What I'm about to share with you is personal. It's who I am behind closed doors. It's who my family is. I'm going to share some practical ways that I build vitality into my life when I'm drained, and I'll discuss boundaries I have put in place to protect myself from exhaustion, fatigue, and failure. I'm guessing many of you will not only relate to the need for renewed vitality but also benefit from some tips on how to get it.

I know we aren't all the same, and what refreshes me may not refresh you. Some of us have much more of a playful spirit, and rest comes easily. Others, like me, are so driven that our minds never fully shut down. Maybe you're in a different category altogether. Maybe your rest doesn't come easily not because you can't cut off the mental noise but because you are at the mercy of a chaotic calendar that owns you. Whatever your personality or approach to ministry, all of us need to build into our lives times of personal and relational renewal, the kind that goes much deeper than a Sunday afternoon nap. Hopefully my suggestions will be a springboard for your thinking and a catapult for your vitality.

SPIRITUAL VITALITY

I know you are tempted to skip this section. I feel a little like I'm wagging my finger and preaching to the choir, to tell you the truth. You and I already know this, right? Sure. Then again, so did all of my peers who have had moral failures recently. Knowing something in our heads doesn't mean we'll live it out in our lives. If we are honest, most of us wake up with an endless list of tasks on our minds, and our intimacy with God often takes a backseat to saving the world.

As a self-proclaimed former workaholic, I know my biggest temptation is not to run off with another woman or embezzle the church's money; it is to run off to save the world and leave my Lord in the dust. Daily I must decide if I want to substitute my work for God for my relationship with God. I'll even go a step further. Pastors are just like everyone else. Nurturing our own spiritual vitality comes no more easily to us than it does to the people we preach to each weekend. I'm not just talking about having a quiet time either. I'm talking about being still long enough to hear the quiet voice of God in our lives. Many of us are guilty of speeding through time with our Father so we can tackle our inbox. How do I know we are all in the same boat? I talk to you. My wife talks to other wives. I see it played out in so many of our lives. We all struggle in this area, but we can choose to change.

Ten years ago I made a promise to God, my wife, and my church: I would give my mornings to God. Consistently. I made a decision to schedule no meetings before lunch. I determined that the best gift I could give to my family and my church was a spiritually healthy me. I started going to bed earlier so I could get up earlier. I am not normally a morning person, but there's no doubt my brain is fresher and has more clarity after seven hours of sleep. I spend

> **Nurturing our own spiritual vitality comes no more easily to us than it does to the people we preach to each weekend.**

time alone in the Word and prayer in the quiet of our home before anyone else gets up. Sometimes I venture out for my own private prayer walk and talk out loud to God in the early morning hours. Other days I write out my concerns and prayers in a journal.

Before I started journaling, I had always been a little ADD about prayer. I couldn't keep my mind going in one direction, and I would get sidetracked and somehow stop talking to God and begin making mental notes, like how I needed more coffee or did I record the latest *College GameDay*? Journaling helps me focus in my prayer life. If I do get sidetracked, I simply write down the unwanted thought so I can remember to take care of it later.

Those early mornings are my uninterrupted time with God. He grabs my heart and mind as I once again submit all of myself to him. This is by no means my time to study for a message or for a speaking engagement. This is wholly different. I'm in my study before the world wakes up so I can build spiritual vitality into my life. Reconnecting with my Father, worshiping him, confessing sin, and praying for others is what it's all about.

I then switch gears and pull my weight around the house. I fix breakfast, hang with the kids, and then take them to school. It only takes about an hour, but I score big brownie points in the marriage department. Afterward, I'm back to the house for several hours of concentrated time set aside to study and prepare to teach God's Word. Since my mind is more creative in the morning, I invest in some major study time before lunch.

This may not sound very radical to you. To be honest, it doesn't sound radical to me either, but it did ten years ago. Ten years ago, either my devotional life and my sermon prep would get crowded out by the incessant needs, emails, meetings, and tasks or I would combine the two, thinking they were the same. Pastors, your study life is not your devotional life. Your message prep is not the same thing as your personal worship time. Do you want to feel God move in your heart? Do you need him to revive you? Worship him with an undivided heart. There's no doubt that at one time I valued the growth of my church over the growth of my relationship with God. My schedule proved it. Not anymore. I have a plan in place to nurture my spiritual vitality. Jesus's plan has finally become my plan: "Very early in the morning, while it was still dark, Jesus got up, left the house and went off to a solitary place, where he prayed" (Mark 1:35 NIV).

EMOTIONAL VITALITY

If spiritual vitality reconnects us to God, then emotional vitality reconnects us to the person he made us to be. Emotional vitality deals with the health of our psyche, our ability to connect and relate to the people around us in positive ways. Our emotional well-being will also determine our outlook on life as well as our level of confidence, vigor, and tenacity. Those who are emotionally refreshed are not teetering on the edge of burnout, nor are they so obsessed with the drive to be better and do more for the wrong reasons.

God never intended for people to become overwhelmed and consumed by one area of life, yet some of us struggle with a one-track mind and tend to lose our ability to live emotionally healthy lives. When that happens, our greatest strengths can become our most limiting weaknesses. What are our strengths? Pastors are pioneers blazing new paths for an old story. We are prophets driven by a holy discontent to speak the truth to a deceived world. However, if we are not healthy emotionally, our desires can create obsessive habits in our lives that devour our time and energy. The result is pastors so engrossed in doing the work of ministry that they have no energy for anything else.

I speak to pastors across the nation at conferences, in coaching networks, and in leadership venues, and I've heard their stories. Most of us don't know how to slow down or shut down. We don't know how to turn off the mental noise. As such, we don't even sleep all that well. Burdens for people, stressful decisions, and anxiety have some of us pacing the floors in the middle of the night. We can't stop thinking about ministry. We may not want to. Passionately pursuing the next creative message idea or planning to launch some innovative ministry might stoke our fire, but it might also rob us of much-needed emotional vitality.

As we talk about our plans with our teams and formulate our vision, some of us fail to see that it's all we talk about. We fail to recognize that we've slipped into a one-track ministry mind. Don't think that's you? Let me ask you some questions: On your last date with your spouse, did you talk about ministry? Were you able to spend time with each other and discuss things other than staffing or vision or church business? I'm guilty of failure here. My wife is my partner in every way, and we have certainly found ourselves robbing our dates to foster our ministry. When we do, we rob our intimacy and friendship. I also rob myself of the vitality I could gain if I would simply unplug for a while. A counselor once encouraged Tricia and I to begin to schedule a one-hour lunch or other meeting where we could hold and release our biggest ministry discussions. It has taken discipline, but it has helped tremendously!

Maybe you can relate. Maybe you don't have a life outside of ministry. Without a hobby or an excuse for a little fun, you might not laugh all that much. Are you stressed out? More mentally fatigued than physically fatigued? Some of us might even admit to an emotional numbness at this moment. Can you believe I just described the average pastor in America? I certainly just described my early ministry years. I did not shut down. I did not stop working. I could not stop thinking about ministry—first by choice, and eventually by habit. I was unaware of how devastating a lack of regular mental Sabbaths was for me and my family.

After those beach talks with Tricia, however, I began to discipline myself. I stopped reading spiritual or leadership books in the evenings, because they made my mind leap into ministry mode. I have learned that I can't check my email, I can't read blogs, and I can't even do much social networking after I get home. If I do, my mind goes to work. Literally. After countless conversations with pastors across the nation, I can attest that most of us are alike. To be sure, we don't all struggle to the same degree or feel the same mental pull, but most of us have a hard time disengaging. We need help. How do we care for our emotions? How do we find rest for our minds? The answer is simple: to disengage from one thing, we need to engage something else.

I have another confession to make: I am forty-one years old, and I love video games. I especially love NCAA Football. I'm proud to say I am currently the champion among all Mountain Lake pastors. The great thing about a video game is that I can't think about anything except what's happening on that screen, so I'm able to disengage mentally from everything else. It gives my mind a break. I don't use it as an excuse to run from problems that must be faced, and I'm not a couch potato. I do, however, reap tons of rewards from thirty to forty-five minutes of mind candy. My perspective on the day's events shifts.

A little mental distance, as opposed to constant attention, can make some inevitable stress more manageable. Oh, the decisions and leadership challenges I face are still there when I finish the game, but I feel much more emotionally ready to tackle them when I've been refreshed. And, of course, the biggest reward comes when I conquer my opponent! I'm sure that emotionally vitalizing endorphins course through my veins every time. I know some of you think I'm crazy, but that's okay. Others of you are already asking yourselves, "What could offer me that kind of mental release?"

Watching movies has the same effect on me as my mind sinks into another story. When I engage in story different than my own, one that might have me laughing out loud or cheering on the underdog, once again my mind is able to disengage and my emotional vitality skyrockets. How did Jesus nurture emotional vitality in his life and the lives of the apostles? Check this: "They went away by themselves in a boat to a solitary place" (Mark 6:32 NIV). Jesus got away from the daily demands with a few good friends, and he relaxed. Maybe, just maybe, he was onto something.

What could it be for you? Maybe it's riding a bike or hiking. For some of you, an afternoon of golf would be gold, or catching a football game with a buddy might do the trick. I know what you're thinking: "We can't afford that." Well, you can't afford emotional numbness either. You, your family, and your ministry cannot afford or sustain your lack of emotional vitality. If it requires going before our church boards and asking for budgeted funds for some hobbies, I believe in it that much. We must find rest for our minds!

RELATIONAL VITALITY

Nurturing relational vitality means nourishing the vibrancy and strength of our personal relationships, and that requires an investment of time and vulnerability.

"I spend time with lots of people," you may think to yourself. You log relational hours in worship services, volunteer meetings, church activities, and staff engagements. You clock even more time counseling individuals or serving in community projects. "Yes," you tell yourself, "I have lots of relationships."

Not so fast. The kind of relationships I'm talking about go much deeper than a chat during a potluck dinner or the handshakes and pats on the back after Sunday services. The hard-hitting truth is that most pastors simply don't engage in deep relationships all that well. There are lots of reasons why.

> **The hard-hitting truth is that most pastors simply don't engage in deep relationships all that well.**

Relationships aren't built in crowds, yet that's where we spend most of our time. In the crowds, conversations stay light and on the surface. "How are you doing?" "Fine." In the crowds, most of our conversations are focused on the other person. "Yes, I'll pray for that need." People in the crowd tend to expect us to have it all together too. They assume our spiritual maturity and wisdom are far greater than their own. And while that may or may not be true, trying to live up to that expectation means we construct relational walls between us and the people we lead. As people pour out their deepest hurts and expose their most secret thoughts and fears, you never let your guard down, never let anyone inside your heart and mind. Many of our experiences in the relationship department are one-sided. These situations don't constitute deep relationships. They represent moments of teaching, leading, and even friendship, but God designed you to need something more, something deeper, something much more personal.

Crowds aren't our only limitation in the relationship arena. Misperceptions of who we are can build walls as well. It's happened to me. I've experienced the change in the social temperature when a new acquaintance discovers that I'm a pastor. They assume that I will wag my finger at their choices or that I am a stick-in-the-mud, so the conversation shuts down and they subtly move away. I've even felt it in past churches I've served. Church members straightened up when another pastor or I would walk in the room. Laughter would end. Subjects would change. Why? Because we were staff and they were laity, and they viewed us as different. It can take months, even years, to break through those misperceptions and show these people we're not out to get them and we're not going to point out their sin to God in case he missed it. Misperceptions like that are part of the reason I wanted to plant a church. I wanted to create a place where people could change the way they thought about church *and* pastors.

Some of us don't have to wait for crowds or mistaken impressions to rob us of relational vitality. We do a fine job of that ourselves. By becoming so wrapped up in tasks and deadlines, we've allowed our ministries to become our job, not our privilege, and the zeal that got us started on this journey has quickly faded. Distinguishing between worship and work becomes harder and harder, resulting in a desire to simply pull back from the body of Christ. We spend time formulating and recruiting for our Sunday school and small group ministries, but the average pastor is not even involved in one. If we are, it's because we feel it's our biblical mandate to attend, not necessarily because we enjoy the biblical community there. Those groups have come to represent "work" in our minds, not life-giving community. After all, we are "on" in those environments, answering questions, praying, drawing others out, casting vision, and, as always, thinking how we could grow the group.

That isn't the only reason we pull away from the body of Christ. Have you ever been maligned or slandered? Has a divisive issue in your church blown up in your face? Or has a person or group of people misunderstood or disagreed with your methods and then caused conflict? Sure, you do what's best for your church, but the damage is done. Betrayal cuts deep and can build relational walls. My wife has talked with countless pastors' wives who secretly struggle with opening themselves up to people after their husbands have been verbally attacked. We aren't the only ones who are tempted to cocoon; our spouses experience burnout and betrayal just like us.

As a result, pastors and ministry leaders are sometimes lonely, isolated, and distrusting, and their relational vitality plummets. Remember, God designed us to be relational—with him and with others—yet many of us are missing out on replenishing relationships, and we're paying the price. Eventually the damage spills into our professional lives with feelings of bitterness, burnout, and apathy.

Try this: study the passages of Scripture regarding all the times Jesus was trying to get away from the crowds to be with just a few close friends. Jesus often withdrew from the masses to hang out with Peter, James, and John. He enjoyed private moments with Lazarus, Mary, and Martha. These were replenishing relationships in his life. They were people he knew, and they knew him too. They loved him. He could share his private thoughts with them, and they revitalized him.

I am ashamed to say that I don't think Tricia and I had a single date during those first two years of church planting. We loved each other and spent almost every waking moment together, but we overlooked how much we needed relaxing time together.

We even thought we had a good excuse. Church planters don't have enough money, right? Wrong. We have since learned that a date can be as simple as a cup of coffee, and nothing is more costly than a prized relationship hitting the skids.

Years ago, during those beach talks, we made commitments to each other to nurture our relational vitality as a couple and as a family by setting aside time just for us. We normally don't do anything overly romantic, although sometimes I surprise her. In fact, while Tricia and I were walking through a department store one night on a date, I was feeling a little guilty that I hadn't planned something more exciting. She deserved more. I asked her, "Doesn't

Date nights don't have to be grandiose, just consistent.

this get old to you? We're just walking around, shopping, running errands, and talking." I'll never forget what she said: "You underestimate what it does for me to simply get away from the world and be with my best friend for a while. I feel closer to you every time." I was reminded once again that date nights don't have to be grandiose, just consistent. Time together fills a need for my wife, but it fills a need for me too. My guard is completely down as I talk, share, laugh, and dream with my wife. Together we build relational vitality. Loneliness and isolation are banished.

Tricia and I also designated one night each week for "family night." Most times, our kids now lay out the plans: Guitar Hero, movie rentals, bike rides, homemade milk shakes, or backyard games they've created. I admit I sometimes don't feel like playing a homemade version of base-soccer-badminton (don't ask), but there's really nothing like acting like a kid again. Goofing off with my family refreshes me more than I realize. God constantly reminds me that family night doesn't have to be spectacular, just scheduled. Pastor, is your family on your schedule? You will schedule what's important to you. Why not schedule your most refreshing relationships as top priority?

Relational vitality isn't limited to family either. Whether it's someone inside your church or ministry area or an old friend from your school days, open the relational doors wide! The point is, make time for it. You were created for it.

INTELLECTUAL VITALITY

I hated school. Correction: I hated studying. Otherwise, school was a blast. Skipping class, cutting up with friends, practical jokes, sports, and parties were the highlights of my academic career, not necessarily cracking the books. Most often, I turned study groups into an excuse to make a burger run with my pals. I became a master at memorizing material the night before a major test, cramming it into my short-term memory just to get a passing grade. I relied on my ability to regurgitate the study guide and slide by with a "good enough" grade. When I graduated, I celebrated. No more tests. No more required reading. No more studying. Or so I thought.

A few years later, I entered vocational ministry with a spitfire attitude. I knew I had some talent as a communicator, and I recognized the gifts that God had given me. That, coupled with experience I gained in lay ministry, gave me a lot of professional energy, and I dove into the world of church work by organizing ministries, teaching, and leading the ever-present church meetings. But that energy only carried me so far. My relational quotient, my communication skills, and my past church experiences weren't any match for the issues I faced. No matter how engaging I might or might not be, sheer personality wasn't enough to overcome the massive problems confronting the church. I had so many questions: *How do I make our church attractive to people who have misconceptions about church? What are the innate growth barriers in our church, and how can we overcome them? How do I lead the staff and hold them accountable while also being their friends? What about finances?* The decisions were daunting.

In my school years, I tended to get by on "good enough," but "good enough" certainly didn't get the job done in ministry. Nor did I want it to. My desire was to honor God, bear much fruit, and make God proud, and I was a quick study in one area: my leadership could make or break a church. The decisions of any ministry leader have far-reaching effects, and I saw those decisions play out as I watched the leaders around me.

Let me give you some examples of how a pastor's abilities or inabilities can make a huge difference in the life of a church. A pastor's ability to resolve conflict in healthy ways has the potential to keep peace in the church at a minimum or avoid a church split in the extreme. What about preaching or teaching skills? Relying on the same messages or even style of delivery has the potential to stalemate the discipleship of the members of the church.

A leader's ability to continue to spread the gospel to the unreached people in the community depends greatly on the ability not only to develop an evangelistic vision for church members but also to create space and interest for the unreached people. And what about all the financial decisions a pastor must make? Unwise choices in this department can cripple a church, thereby limiting the work of God as the church faces the consequences of a lack of monetary resources.

Now, all of these revelations didn't hit me on day one of my ministry career, but it definitely didn't take long for me to grasp the gravity of my position as a lead pastor. I came face-to-face with my distinct need to equip myself to be far better than "good enough." My revelations weren't solely rooted in observations either. Paul challenged Timothy to prepare and equip himself for the work ahead: "Do your best to present yourself to God as one approved, a worker who does not need to be ashamed and who correctly handles the word of truth. . . . All Scripture is God-breathed and is useful for teaching, rebuking, correcting and training in righteousness, so that the servant of God may be thoroughly equipped for every good work" (2 Tim. 2:15; 3:16–17 NIV).

Paul had a point. His admonishments to train, prepare, and arm ourselves are ones we would be wise to take seriously. Following this advice is what I call intellectual vitality.

My ministry story is rather typical. Many of us tend to rely too heavily on talent, experience, basic know-how, and the successes of our pasts rather than "cracking the books." Pursuing intellectual vitality—studying leadership resources and developing a skill set to match our ministry tasks—takes discipline and effort that many may disdain. It requires creating a personal growth plan, reading resources on topics ranging from leadership to character development, listening to sermons by other pastors, and evaluating our own progress consistently and honestly.

The tyranny of the urgent keeps us from developing our strengths and improving our weaknesses. Over time, too many of us get mentally flabby. We stop growing as preachers. We stop growing as leaders. As a result, our congregations suffer as we offer our brand of "good enough" ministry and vision. The consequences of our poor decisions or waffling ideas wreak havoc on the people we lead—or fail to lead.

Once again, let me give you some personal, practical tips for increasing intellectual vitality. In my time with the Lord these days, I read from his Word, but I also try to read books on preaching, ecclesiology, leadership, and management. My bookshelves are full of resources representing hours and hours of intellectual vitality. I listen to podcasts of great preaching regularly for both spiritual growth and fresh perspectives on God's Word. Most days while getting ready to leave the house, I'm listening to someone else's preaching. I don't just listen to and read from people who agree with me either. That wouldn't help me grow.

I also work diligently to plan out a six- to nine-month teaching calendar. I've asked my ministry team to help hold me accountable on this. Creating a teaching calendar keeps our church and team fresh as we brainstorm to plan creative elements, and it keeps me from falling back into old patterns of procrastination and knee-jerk sermons. I schedule my sermon preparation first on my calendar, and nothing interrupts it. I realize that I must put in the necessary time to listen to God so I can bring a fresh word from the Lord each week.

While I value conferences and seminars and attend several of them each year, I plan ahead to connect with pastors and friends around the edges of the conference schedule. I also use these times to create relationships with a few leaders I admire and respect but don't yet know. Spending one-on-one time with other leaders often sharpens me more than listening to a conference speaker teach to hundreds. In these more intimate sessions, I can share specifics of my story and gain insightful feedback. Reaching out to and scheduling time with mentors requires diligence, of course, but it's so worth it!

Mentoring relationships are an incredible avenue to intellectual vitality for me. One of the secrets to my ministry's success and my own sanity has been the relationships I have with godly, wise leaders and mentors. I have been personally mentored by great leaders such as Andy Stanley, Rick Warren, Sam Chand, Larry Osborne, Alan Hirsch, Greg Surratt, Dan Reiland, Dave Travis, and the list goes on.

How did I develop relationships with these great leaders? Dan Reiland is a good example. Dan is a stellar leader. He was John Maxwell's executive pastor for over twenty years before partnering with John to move INJOY Stewardship Solutions to Atlanta. Currently, he is the executive pastor for 12Stone Church in Lawrenceville, Georgia, one of the fastest-growing churches in America. Needless to say, he has a lot he could teach me.

In 1999, when I moved to the Atlanta area to start our church, I walked up to Dan at a break during an INJOY conference and said, "Dan, you don't know me, but I am a church planter. I'm starting a new church here in Atlanta, and I'm clueless in terms of what it means to lead a church. I believe I have some raw leadership gifts that just need to be developed and sharpened. Could I buy you a cup of coffee and pick your brain about how I might do that most effectively?" Crazy enough, he agreed. We've been friends ever since. Conversations with him have altered the course of my life and ministry.

Many times I have left conversations with great men like Dan with "permission" to be what God has called me to be and do what God has called me to do. Don't be afraid to ask for guidance from some leaders who have gone ahead of you. Many are more than willing to invest their time and energy into you and your leadership potential.

Coaching relationships and networks have also allowed me to learn from other pastors and churches. Since our church began, I have sought out numerous networking relationships with pastors. In the early years of my church planting career, I secured a friend's beach condo and invited a few of my church planting friends. We split the grocery bills and talked about ministry for two days. Those days shaped our churches and helped form some of my best ministry friendships to date! Since that time, I have joined groups like Leadership Network's Learning Communities as well as Future Travelers, a group of pastors I connect with a few times each year. In those gatherings, we envision the future of the church together and brainstorm creative ways to reach people who are disconnected from Christ and his church.

The key to maintaining these types of mentoring and networking relationships is intentionality. Pastors are busy people. Who isn't? We're tempted to assume we don't have enough time to pull away from our daily agenda, or we can't imagine adding one more appointment to the calendar. Yet each time I get pastors into these settings, they tell me that these conversations fuel them! I have heard it said that we change primarily through the influence of the people we know and the books we read. I know that's true for me. I have never had an original thought! Because of my relationships and the resources I am consistently exposed to, I don't need to. I simply observe, listen, contextualize, and execute.

How are you growing as a leader, a pastor, and a communicator of God's Word? Zeal is simply not enough to carry us through ministry and leadership. We must be fully equipped to shepherd God's people. We must grow ourselves. Grow the leader, grow the ministry.

> Zeal is simply not enough to carry us through ministry and leadership. We must be fully equipped to shepherd God's people.

PHYSICAL VITALITY

Remember our definition of vitality? To possess vitality is to possess strength, vibrancy, and health. For a few years I overlooked the importance of physical health as I focused much more on what I was doing with my mind, but I learned in a pretty embarrassing way that physical vitality matters.

At thirty years old, I took an online test that claimed it could calculate my "real age." This was not my chronological age but the actual age of my body, taking into consideration the wear and tear on my muscles, my stress level, and my overall well-being. As I described my lifestyle and habits, the guilt set in. Had I really not been to the dentist in two years? No, I didn't exercise. Yes, I ate fast food more than once a week. Eight hours of sleep each night? Come on. When I clicked the "calculate" button, I cringed. I was shocked to learn that my body's "real age" was ten years older than I really was!

My shock turned to disgust when my wife's real age came in younger—a lot younger. Now my competitive drive kicked in, and I got motivated to change. I had not noticed that I was getting soft in the gut or lacked energy. Those kinds of things usually happen without you noticing. That test, however, put a spotlight on the issue. I didn't become a fitness fanatic, but I did create some new habits, and over time my physical health drastically improved. Recently I took the same real age test again. Now my real age is ten years *younger* than I really am. Do that math. I have actually added twenty years to my life!

These days I exercise much more, I eat far fewer Quarter Pounders, and I have lost almost thirty pounds and kept them off! I am stronger, healthier, and more energetic than I was ten years ago. I will be relevant longer and withstand the requirements of ministry longer because I work hard at nurturing my own physical vitality. I fall off the wagon sometimes, but when I do I get back up and get going again. Numerous people have noticed, by the way. I had a family tell me once, "Just so you know, we are physical therapists, and we joined this church because you seem to model a physically disciplined lifestyle. We've had a hard time finding a church where that was the case." Wow. Who knew people would size up a pastor and his influence based on that?

Physical vitality is critical for more than just our appearance. If it was only about appearance, I would not even address it. Your physical vitality will carry you through your ministry years. It is no secret that we, as pastors and ministry leaders, endure stress, emotional strain, and spiritual burdens. Our physical health—or lack of good health—could radically affect our ability to obey God as we lead our churches. We can't squander the years God gives us. We must be good stewards of the body he has given us. As an added bonus, our spouses will probably like a chiseled temple too!

While I don't necessarily think a perfectly balanced life should be a measure of our success, I wholeheartedly believe that nurturing our vitality in these areas will keep us fighting the good fight longer, stronger, and healthier and bearing more fruit along the way. That's success.

INSIGHT

Mark Batterson, author of ID: The True You *and lead pastor of National Community Church in Washington, DC*

Are you doing ministry out of the overflow of what God is doing in your own heart? If you are, ministry is pure joy. If you aren't, ministry will eat you alive. Your primary responsibility as a leader is your own spiritual development. If you're growing in the spiritual disciplines and in your love for Jesus, everything else will take care of itself. Don't worry about church growth. Church growth is a byproduct of personal growth.

One of the biggest mistakes pastors make is trying to be all things to all people. If you try to be all things to all people, you'll end up being nothing to nobody. You need to put boundaries in your life that guard you, your family, and your time.

Here are a few exhortations:

1. Use all of your vacation days! You owe it to your family and you owe it to your church.

2. Make sure you have a day or days during the week when you don't schedule meetings. I call them focus days. Those are the days I meet with God, study for messages, and feed the vision God has given me.

3. Put your family first. For me that means scheduling no more than one evening meeting a week. Why? Because I need to be there for them. I need to coach teams and help with homework.

4. If your sermons are boring, maybe it's because your life is boring. Get a life outside of church! Find an outlet. Take up a new hobby. Hang out with people who don't go to your church.

5. Guard your day off religiously.

6. If you aren't delegating, you're dying! You should know less and do less as the church grows. And the beautiful thing about that is this: you can't take the credit for what God is doing. One of the greatest joys of ministry is seeing people grow in their gifting. If you aren't delegating, you are robbing someone of that opportunity!

7. Seek out a mentor who is older and wiser. If you can't find a mentor, pay a counselor! You need a sounding board in your life.

QUESTIONS FOR MEASUREMENT

1. What does it mean to "nurture vitality"?

2. Of the different areas of vitality, which one would you say you feel most successful in right now?

3. Which area of vitality do you feel you struggle with the most?

4. What is your reaction to the statement, "One area of discipline flows over into the next"? What could this look like for you?

5

THE MOST FORGOTTEN METRIC

WHAT ARE WE REALLY CALLED TO DO?

I wish I could say I've stumbled onto some new, deep, mystical truth that would fix all of us as pastors. Something so profound that no human has thought of it before. Something so revolutionary that God has waited until now to reveal exactly how we should define ministry success. I haven't. Instead, what I am about to share with you is really, really old news. It's not provocative or even cutting-edge. Make no mistake, however: what I am about to tell you is big. In fact, it probably means life or death for you, your family, and your ministry.

Some of us in ministry leadership have been spinning our wheels to measure up to our self-imposed definition of success by gauging numerical growth too obsessively or by trying to model ourselves and our leadership after some other pastor who has caught our attention. Or maybe we've gotten lost in a long list of ministry tasks because we think success is checking those tasks off our to-do lists. In so doing, we've overlooked our most important task. Pastors and ministry leaders are not immune to losing sight of the goal. As a matter of fact, some of us have not only lost sight but substituted our own goal for God's. In short, we have forgotten God's most important command for all of his followers, the only measure of true success: love.

" 'Love the LORD your God with all your heart, all your soul, and all your mind.' This is the first and greatest commandment. A second is equally important: 'Love your neighbor as yourself' " (Matt. 22:37–39). Jesus said it all comes down to one thing: love for God and love for people. Oh, sure. We know this. We preach this all the time, right? If only our church members could grasp this idea, we could have such a profound effect on the world. Church conflict would never happen. Divorce statistics would plummet among believers. Mass evangelism would result. Needs would be met. Communities would be served. Poverty would not exist.

But to whom was Jesus speaking in Matthew 22? He was speaking to religious people, the spiritual leaders of the day. He was engaging Pharisees who knew the Shema backward and forward, who were master expositors of the Scriptures, who were disciplined and obedient, but who were also poor lovers of people. In their zeal to create a holy nation for God, the Pharisees imposed backbreaking laws and stipulations to guarantee that sin would not prevail among God's people, but they overlooked the need to show God's love to those very people. They became taskmasters rather than representatives of God. In short, Jesus indicted the ministry leaders of his day for a lack of love.

Is it possible that we pastors and ministry leaders are the modern-day Pharisees, but in a different way? We're not counting how many steps Christians take on Sunday, but it is entirely possible that we view people as a means to an end just as the Pharisees did. Their end? To create a perfect, blameless nation. Our end? To create a successful ministry. Either way, success was the goal, and we measure it just as incorrectly today as the Pharisees did back then.

Consider this line of thought for a moment. We deal with people on a daily basis, but often our agenda is not to meet their needs or deepen their understanding of God. Instead, our agenda is to recruit those people to fill volunteer positions in our churches. We assimilate people into service **Some of us are brilliant thinkers, leaders, and teachers but poor lovers of people.** and groups and leadership, yet many of us fail to love them. Rather than getting to know them—the hurts from their past, the demands of their daily lives, or even the activity of God in their lives—we might be guilty of treating them as merely additions to our number of members, volunteers, and leadership heads in order for the ministries of our church to flourish. Some of us are brilliant thinkers, leaders, and teachers but poor lovers of people.

A pastor friend, whose church resided in the same town as a large denomination's seminary, said to me recently, "Shawn, the young men who are attending seminary and serving in my church know how to exposit Scripture brilliantly, but they just don't like people. Some of them have even told me so." Quite the indictment, don't you think?

To be sure, many pastors and ministry leaders don't struggle to love people. Details and tasks don't hinder them from spending countless hours shepherding people, and I admire their endurance. I am not indicting the whole of our profession by any means, but I am convinced that I'm not the only one who has struggled to remain focused on God's definition of success, and our silence or failure to address the issue is costing the kingdom the fruit of our potential.

Here's my assessment: most of us simply don't believe deep down that the Great Commandment is all that great. Otherwise, it would be *the* great pursuit of our lives and ministries. If the Great Commandment motivated us, love for God and people would be the absolute measure of our success. Love would be our number one goal. For some of us, it is not. Instead, we have substituted our love for people with our love of growth and crowds. They have become the measure of ministry success and even the measure of our self-worth. That is why we feel so close to God on crowded Sundays like Easter and Christmas, but we feel as if God has forsaken us on those low number days like on Memorial Day and Fourth of July weekends. That's why we get a sick feeling when some famous pastor tweets about a thousand people getting baptized in one day. We feel inadequate in comparison. We have wrapped up our worth as a spiritual leader in something other than God's definition of success.

My home office is full of books geared toward shedding light on the numbers issue. The market for that type of information is staggering, and rightly so. Numbers mean people, and people are our goal. Yet, if we aren't careful, we slip into a constant pursuit of the next new system or church model that will help us break through the next growth barrier. Is it missional? Is it attractional? Is it organic? What model works best?

When our focus has slipped too far to this extreme, we can find ourselves leaning more on a model or system than on the one who promises to bless his church. I agree that healthy models and church systems can aid us in accomplishing our mission, but I have also noticed that the pendulum sometimes swings too far toward human effort. At Churchplanters.com, pastors will often inquire about the strategy we use at Mountain Lake to run our small groups or guest services areas. They usually want to know which church we're modeled after. The answer is never short and sweet. In fact, I usually begin talking about what I call "the myth of models." Let me explain.

If church history proves anything, it's that the next church system or model will not fix the problems, the sin, and the hurt in our churches. Only Jesus, his love, and his power can do that. Do you remember when you first fell in love with Jesus? Do you remember first understanding that he really is the answer to your every need? What about when you first answered his call to ministry? When he filled you with his overwhelming desire to lead and teach on his behalf, didn't you recognize that he is the head of his church?

I bet you can remember thinking that you wanted to change the way church work was carried out. There were wrongs you wanted to correct. Whether it was the way business meetings sucked the life out of everyone or the way the church service lacked energy, I bet you had a passion to show the world the relevance of Jesus and his ways. Yet somehow over time we get caught up in those same issues and maybe even forget our first love. Maybe we neglect it. We have certainly underestimated it.

Just like the Pharisees who lived in Jesus's day, somewhere in the process we have forsaken love. Pastors, we must stop chasing models and start chasing Jesus again! The health of God's church depends on it. There is no secret model or system that can guarantee success. It's a myth. Only Jesus can draw people to himself. Not even well-thought-out plans can accomplish what only he is capable of doing. Remember what he teaches us: "I am the way and the truth and the life. No one comes to the Father except through me" (John 14:6 NIV).

Am I saying that we should stop trying to grow our churches? No! Jesus told us to go and reach as many people as possible with the gospel. Systems and church models can aid us in our work. They prevent us from losing track of people when the crowds grow large, and they track our progress, helping us see our blind spots. Systems and models often afford us the creativity and administration we need to reach out to our communities, but we must guard ourselves from putting our trust in human plans rather than in the work of the Spirit. We simply can't allow ourselves to forget who holds the power and who determines whether people will be added to our congregations. If you haven't already faced the temptation to take your eyes off Jesus in this area, you likely will at some point in your ministry.

Our problem is nothing new. It dates all the way back to the first century. Remember the church at Ephesus? They had great stuff going on. They were busy. They were growing. However, one thing had been overlooked: "Yet I hold this against you: You have forsaken your first love. Remember the height from which you have fallen! Repent and do the things you did at first. If you do not repent, I will come to you and remove your lampstand from its place" (Rev. 2:4–5 NIV 1984).

Notice who's threatening the church here. It is not Satan. Jesus is the one threatening to remove the lampstand from its place if they keep forsaking love. Could it be that the reason our churches are not healthy or seeing spiritual fruit is not because Satan is attacking us but because Jesus has removed our lampstand because we have forsaken love?

A comprehensive reading of the New Testament reminds us that the church must be more than an organization, a system, or a business. The church is first and foremost a group of people whom Jesus loves. The very mark of following him is our love for his people: "Your love for one another will prove to the world that you are my disciples" (John 13:35). Therefore, love must be the root of every model or plan for church structure. While my church is not backing away from our commitment to reach people, I am evaluating our motivation. Love will be our goal. We will launch new worship services, start new campuses, and plant new churches. We will send hundreds of people around the world to love people in the name of Jesus Christ each year. We will most definitely "go and tell." I believe in the Great Commission, and I am certainly not saying we should stop pursuing it. What I am saying, however, is that we must stop pursuing the Great Commission at the expense of the Great Commandment. We must stop using people to get ministry done. People are our ministry.

Why am I telling you all of this? I don't want you to make the same mistakes I have made. In my ministry journey, love has often not been my number one goal. At times I have used people to accomplish ministry. At times I have measured my success, my sense of significance, and my self-worth by the nickels and noses in my church. I have had days when I was so focused on the next ministry task that I blew right past the person God

> **We must stop using people to get ministry done. People are our ministry.**

had placed in front of me. I am ashamed to say that I have forsaken the Great Commandment more than any other commandment for much of my ministry. But God is good in spite of my weaknesses, and he has been doing a new work in my life. God is teaching me to love people with his kind of love. He is creating within me a new heart.

Let me tell you what he's been doing in me. I enjoy being with people more these days. Sound like I must have led a jaded life? Not really. I love the people I serve, but too often I viewed them as just that. I didn't take advantage of the friendships and relationships that were right in front of me. Maybe you'd be willing to admit the same thing. Maybe you too are guilty of serving without loving. Thanks be to God, I have found a new love for hanging out in the church lobby on the weekends, shaking hands and hugging necks. I look forward to the one-on-one encounters. I am learning how to pay more attention to the person in front of me rather than the next task ahead of me. My ADD sometimes gets the better of me, but God is teaching me to be still and love.

I love my small group now. They are not just a responsibility anymore. They are becoming some of my best friends. Yes, I actually have friends in my church! Imagine that. I'm investing in smaller groups of people these days and encouraging their faith. I'm watching my staff grow spiritually and professionally, and I am seeking ways to mentor and challenge them. I even look forward to going to volunteer team meetings now, not simply because of the work that we'll accomplish but also because those teams are made up of real people with real hurts who work forty to sixty hours per week and then come to every meeting we have. We don't pay them. We actually ask them to bring money with them every Sunday. Church is not their only life, however. They have concerns. They have pain. They have questions. They need to be loved. God has renewed my perspective regarding the people I lead, and I have been humbled.

I have a heightened desire to pray for people these days. I have always prayed—mostly about me. For a long time my prayers were all about me, my ministry, and our church's concerns. Since God has begun this new work in my heart, I am much more aware of the needs of the people around me, and I pray for them by name throughout the day. I catch myself praying as I drive through my neighborhood for those who attend my church and even those who don't. God is softening my heart. I cry more these days as I'm often moved by the hurts in my church. Yes, I have always cared about the people I pastor, but God is taking me to a deeper understanding of what it means to bear one another's burdens the way the New Testament teaches.

I am certainly not bragging about all of this. Actually, I am quite ashamed to confess that my heart has not always been this soft. It's one thing to confess to a trusted confidant but quite another to publish that confession. I pray my confession might resonate with some of you, and you too would pray for God to do a new work in your heart.

I'm encouraged by God's activity in my heart. God is reminding me that neither my success nor my spiritual growth is measured by improvement in my preaching, my skill in leading, or the size and influence of my church, but only by the growth of my love! I am on the journey to becoming content with measuring success the way God does. God is teaching me that at the end of the day, only one thing will make me successful. Only one thing will make me significant. Only one thing will make me stand out from the rest of the world. It's not being cool, casual, contemporary, or creative. It's not my brilliant preaching or the size of my church. Jesus said, "Your love for one another will prove to the world that you are my disciples" (John 13:35). Love is all that matters to him. Love is what makes me a disciple. Love is success. Love is the essence of the Christian life. There is nothing deeper than that.

> **Love is the essence of the Christian life. There is nothing deeper than that.**

Can you imagine what would happen if you began to measure success the way God does? Do you think it is possible that the drive, the discouragement, and the discontent that we talked about in chapter 1 could melt away? Can you imagine the loneliness and insecurity fading? Here's the good news: if the church at Ephesus is any indication, love really is all we need.

Here is even better news: Do you know what people are attracted to in the world today? It is not video screens, contemporary music, casual dress, and coffee. That grabs attention, but it doesn't grab hearts. People are attracted to love. Love never goes out of style, and it never becomes irrelevant. God's love is attractional and missional. It's even organic. If we, as pastors and ministry leaders, would return to love, could it be that God might grant the desires for growth and influence that he has actually planted in our hearts? Loving people is the best way to show a watching world who he is. When our churches—beginning with us—are built on love, our buildings won't be able to hold the crowds that are drawn to experience it.

Let's go back and do the things we did at first. Let's return to our original calling and remember why we got into ministry in the first place. Let's show the world the love of Christ—not just the love he showed on the cross, but the love he wants to share through us. If we do, we will be successful in his eyes. Isn't that all we really want?

INSIGHT

Matt Carter, pastor of preaching and vision,
The Austin Stone Community Church

Shawn hits the nail on the head here. As the pastor of a church that has been blessed to see a lot of growth in the past nine years, I have had to keep my motivations for ministry in check. It can be easy to get caught up in tracking attendance, giving, and the number of volunteers you have serving. While paying attention to those numbers isn't bad in and of itself, it can make you lose sight of what should be our first love—Jesus. I don't want to lose sight of my love for Christ. We run the risk that if we fall more in love with our mission than with our Savior, then our Savior will have no part in our mission.

We see an example of this in Revelation 2 with the church at Ephesus. This church is commended for their works, their toil, and their endurance yet is in jeopardy of having its lampstand removed—so that Jesus would then have no part of this church. Wow! What did they do to deserve this stern warning?

Well, we see in verse 4 that they abandoned their first love. They abandoned their love for Christ and their love for one another. So despite all their typically praiseworthy activities, they are scolded for their lack of love. God doesn't just command us to love him and to love one another; he expects it of us. So while we should desire to see our churches grow, to see more people attending worship services, to see more people baptized, and to see more people serving the local body, we must be careful that this desire for growth doesn't supersede our desire for love. We should always love our Savior more than we love our mission.

When working with our staff and volunteer leaders, we talk about how we don't use people to get tasks or ministry done; we use tasks and ministry to get people done. What we mean by that is that we have a chance to disciple, sharpen, and show love to our people while they are accomplishing ministry tasks. We have a chance to point people to the love of Christ through the way we model our personal love for him and the way we show love to others.

QUESTIONS FOR MEASUREMENT

1. What do you think it means to "use people to get ministry done"?

2. Would you say you pursue relationships more for the interests of others or for your own interests?

3. How could focusing more on the needs of people around you impact your current weekly schedule?

4. How do you think investing in people at a deeper level would impact your ministry?

6

SUCCESS IS
SPELLED TEAM

Pastors generally don't work well on teams. We are entrepreneurial. We are self-starters. We are often the strongest leaders in the room. We like to make decisions, not necessarily wait for someone else to make them. Through Churchplanters.com, I have had the opportunity to gather hundreds of pastors together each year and witness the dynamic firsthand.

As pastors, we have ideas, philosophies, and—let's admit it—opinions. We are also extremely busy people, often wearing lots of hats. And if we were all completely honest, we might admit that we find it difficult to slow down long enough to allow a team of other people to assist us in ministry. Being part of a team might force us to take additional time to talk through various ideas or explain the details, and, well, we just don't have time for that. We operate from the "I'll just make the decision, and then we'll move on" philosophy.

Sometimes we are right. We could make the call without consulting the team. Sometimes we could save everyone the hassle and fly solo. Sometimes not. Being a great leader doesn't necessarily make us a great team player, even when we need to be. Some of the greatest leaders in the church whom I know personally are somewhat difficult to work with and for, and I would include myself in that description.

Before we heap abuse on ourselves, though, let's take a little solace from the apostle Paul. He struggled with the team concept. Most of his team didn't make the full run with him. He lost team members like Phygelus and Hermogenes (see 2 Tim. 1:15) and Demas (see 2 Tim. 4:10). He even once had a big blowup with Barnabas over John Mark, another team member (see Acts 15:36–40). Leading a team is not always easy, no matter how much you love Jesus! One of the great challenges I have faced since entering the ministry is leading the inner circle team that God has entrusted to my care.

However, our success in ministry will largely rise and fall based on our team. We need a team—a great team—if we want to be and do everything God wants for us. Jesus had a great team. No one realized it at the time, but he did. His team was eager to learn and willing to serve. His team passionately loved him. His team did whatever it took to get the job done. If Jesus needed a killer team to accomplish what God had called him to do, then we probably do too.

You've almost certainly heard the acronym TEAM: Together Everyone Accomplishes More. It's so true in the church. For us to accomplish the vision God has for us, we don't simply need to become better leaders. We must become better team leaders. Leadership always involves people. Success is revealing God's vision to people and winning their wholehearted support. Making disciples requires leading, teaching, serving, loving, and praying. It requires a team! Without a doubt, we must take people with us. As leaders, we must learn to operate within the context of a team to fully accomplish all that God has asked of us. I love John Maxwell's favorite leadership proverb: "He who thinks he leads, but has no followers, is only taking a walk."[1] Proverbs 14:28 from *The Message* says it this way: "The mark of a good leader is loyal followers; leadership is nothing without a following."

The bottom line is that our success hinges on whether we effectively lead our team. Everything rises and falls on our team leadership culture. As goes the team, so goes the organization. As pastors and ministry leaders, we must invest not just in the masses but also in the team God has entrusted to us. By remaining accessible to our team, helping to nurture their vitality, and developing their skills, we will ultimately further the mission of the church we lead. We owe a lot to our team. Many of these men and women give their all to serve and love people in our churches. Just as it was with Jesus, our team is our first ministry responsibility.

> **Just as it was with Jesus, our team is our first ministry responsibility.**

What could we offer the people on our teams that would help us accomplish his mission together? I truly believe that some focused attention in a few areas will result in exponential fruit. So what should our teams expect from us?

CHARACTER

Character matters. Charisma will take us only so far. We can't be all talk; our character must be solid. Having character doesn't mean we'll perfectly lead without flaw. It just means we will consistently live out the qualities and characteristics of Jesus. Pastors and ministry leaders ought to model a way of life and a level of integrity worthy of being followed. That is a serious responsibility. Character must be a measure of our success. Without godly character, we ultimately fail to honor God.

The word *integrity* means "a sound, unimpaired, or perfect condition." When a clay pot is baked in an oven, if it is baked too long or if the clay is substandard, the pot can develop cracks. Sometimes these cracks are very tiny, perhaps even impossible to see. Once they are there, however, they only grow. They don't go away. Over time, the cracks grow and eventually break the pot, and whatever is inside spills out all over the place. So when you buy a clay pot, you want one without cracks, one that has integrity. Someone trying to sell a pot without integrity might try to paint over the cracks, but covering over the flaws won't prevent the damage that cracks can cause.

I so passionately want my life to be a life without concealed cracks. I don't want to paint over flaws, hoping the cracks won't ever be exposed. The very idea that we would try to hide character flaws and secret sins proves that we often measure success by what people think about us more than by what God thinks about us. That hits me hard.

Character is a life without concealed cracks. The truth is that none of us are perfectly seamless; we all have a few cracks. Recognizing them and repenting of them, even to our team, can help build our credibility and leadership effectiveness with the teams we lead. Consistency between my public life and my private life has become even more important for me, and it is something I work toward diligently. Today there is less of a gap between the public persona and the private sectors of my life. God deserves that. My team deserves that.

One staff member who spent over a decade with me before God called him on to other fields told me as he neared his departure, "Shawn, even in the times when I disagreed with you, when I would have done it another way, or when I might have been frustrated with you, I have never questioned your motives.

I have never questioned your heart. I have always believed you were seeking to hear from God." That is the best compliment I could have been paid. From my team member's perspective, my character made me worthy to follow. Character must be a measure of success not just from the pulpit but behind the scenes too.

CARE

People don't care what you know until they know that you care. This is so true when it comes to leading a team. To lead any team effectively, we must care for the individuals on the team. But with so much on our plates as pastors and ministry leaders, we often don't show our love and support all that well. Our tendency is to value excellence in our programming over the needs of our team. Our tendency is to use people to get ministry done. The great temptation for those of us who are highly driven is to overlook the personal lives of the people on our teams and focus only on the contribution they make to the team. In so doing, we fail to love and care for them the way they absolutely deserve. The result just might be a wake of destruction left behind us while we forge ahead to change the

> **Our tendency is to value excellence in our programming over the needs of our team.**

world for Jesus. I am not accusing; I'm just pointing out the temptation. I have certainly been tempted to run ahead and forget the helpers God has given me. At times I have cared for my team well at Mountain Lake. Other times I have been so busy, moving so quickly, that I have blown right past the people closest to me.

I highly doubt many of us have intentions of blowing right by our teams. I really don't believe that most of us intend to let our relationships with team members decay. One pastor said to

me, "My worship pastor and I just aren't on the same page."
He went on to talk about the small tug-of-war the two were
playing regarding the structure and intention of their weekly
worship services. I then asked him this question: "What does
your weekly meeting with him look like?"

"Well," he said, "we don't really have a scheduled weekly
meeting time. We are so busy running in different directions.
I do a ton of counseling and juggle a crazy schedule, and it's
just so hard to find the time to actually meet." I have had
virtually the same discussion with dozens, if not hundreds, of
senior pastors across America. Not having enough time for
our team is a cop-out. If we want to lead our team effectively,
we must spend time with and demonstrate care for our team!
If we want to be and stay on the same page, we must prioritize
time with them.

All that being said, I haven't met many pastors who simply
don't care about their teams. I think that most of the time our
care just gets lost in the shuffle of overcrowded schedules and
overloaded lives. If our efforts to care for them are haphazard
and only happen when things slow down, we will never care for
our teams. The biggest challenge is prioritizing and building
systems of care in and around the teams we lead.

At Mountain Lake we have tried to make demonstrating care
a natural rhythm of ministry. First of all, every Tuesday morning, the only exception to no morning meetings I have, is probably the most important meeting of the week for our team. We
currently call it "FBT," which stands for "Fist Bump Tuesday."
The sole purpose of this meeting is to give each other "fist
bumps" of encouragement from the previous week of ministry.
We drink coffee and snack together while we simply encourage each other and spur one another on. We used to call this
meeting "MoJo's"—the "Mo" was for Monday, "Jo" was for
coffee. I later found that my team of driven self-starters would
rather hit the ground running Monday and then pull back a

notch the next morning, making a team meeting of this nature more feasible for them.

No matter the name, the place, or the time, the purpose of the meeting is simple: encouragement and praise. Having witnessed each other doing some things right during the previous week, we give out fist bumps to each other based on the execution of our mission. We commend and encourage one another based on specific ways we have served our team or our church. We celebrate the ministry home runs we have seen each other hit in our particular areas of leadership, and we take time to notice the strides we are making personally and professionally. We also focus on spiritual and leadership development, taking time to highlight those who are reaching new heights in either area. This is the time when I ask God to put fuel back in the tanks of my team members. I highly value this meeting, and it is required for all full-time staff because they absolutely need to know that they are valued and appreciated.

Recently, my wife uploaded a "Team 411" spreadsheet to our office network and shared it with every member of our team. The spreadsheet highlights vital information for each of our team members: birthdays, wedding anniversaries, employment anniversaries, favorite restaurants, favorite meals, favorite coffees or drinks, favorite candy/snacks, favorite pastimes, favorite sports teams, and even favorite flowers (for ladies, of course!). With this information, we are better equipped to speak a team member's love language the next time they need a pick-me-up. We've even used it to plot random acts of kindness for each other! Demonstrating love in tangible ways is another way we care for those closest to us.

By the way, our small groups pastor does the same type of thing with his small group leaders. Our children's pastor does the same thing with his volunteers. We are creating a culture of care in our leadership teams at Mountain Lake, and the people are better for it. They know their contribution is appreciated, and they feel valued. Caring about leaders for more than what we can get out of them must be a measure of success.

Accessibility is another way we can communicate care to our teams. Overcrowded agendas often mean preachers stay behind closed doors or booked with other appointments much of the time. This makes us largely inaccessible to our teams. My team knows that they can call me, email me, or come by to see me, and they will not be an interruption to my ministry. How do they know? Because I have told them.

I do block off some uninterrupted time each day for studying when everyone knows I need to not be disturbed, but the rest of the day my team knows they can get in touch with me. They rarely get sent to voice mail. Most of my appointments are booked weeks in advance. My team knows, however, that if someone on my team needs me, I am available. We can usually find a way to meet that day or the next. My team is important to me, and I tell them so. I want my team to know that they have my attention. Why? These men and women are helping me carry the load of ministry, and few other people understand the burdens they bear and the spiritual battles they face. I do. As a matter of fact, I'm leading them into many of those battles. I want them to be better men and women because of the time spent under my care. Caring for my team is a measure of my success!

CLARITY

There is something else our teams deserve from us as their leaders: clarity. We don't intend to, but we often focus on our vision for the masses and neglect to reveal that vision to our team. We wrongly assume they just "get it." As the team leader, we must make sure the vision is clear among our team members.

What is the mission statement of your organization or ministry? Can you recite it word for word without looking at it?

Could everyone on your team recite your mission word for word? Before you answer, ask every team member separately to write down the mission of your organization (without looking it up). Then, at your next meeting, have each one recite aloud the mission of your church. You might 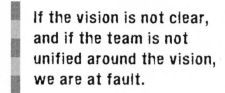 **If the vision is not clear, and if the team is not unified around the vision, we are at fault.** come to realize that you have not been as clear as you think you have been about the vision for the ministry of your church. If the vision is not clear, and if the team is not unified around the vision, we are at fault. We are the leaders! Pastors, give yourself to the cause of unifying your team around God's great vision for the church. Clarity and unity must be a measure of our success!

Our teams also deserve clarity about the expectations we have for them. How can they hit the target if they don't know what it is? Mapping out distinct goals and setting definitive project deadlines gives everyone a clear understanding of what the expectations are. As the team leader, think through things like office environment (what people wear and how the office should be organized) and team culture (how members relate to each other) as well as job performance (hitting deadlines, attention to detail, and getting the job done). Determine what you expect of your team, and then make it clear. Say it. Write it down. Schedule team member reviews as often as necessary. Hold everyone accountable to meeting the expectations.

What's the only thing worse than a team member not knowing where the target is? A leader who either doesn't know or can't communicate where the target is. Without clear expectations, team members won't have the chance to experience the thrill of a job well done. Instead, they will characterize their service as chaos—always tweaking this or that but never quite knowing what the goal was. Our teams deserve the chance to do their jobs well. Leaders, help them. Clearly define the objective. And remember, clarity in this area isn't only a benefit to the team member. It certainly benefits us as we evaluate and review job performances. Clarity of expectation must be a measure of our success.

CONVICTION

Passion and authority. These are the things Jesus brought to his team. We have too many pastors who are complainers and not enough pastors with conviction. We have too many pastors who are good at exegesis but lack passion and authority. Pastors, once we have spent time with God, we must speak for God to our teams! We must be passionate about what we do. We need to let our teams know we love our jobs. They need to see us sit up on the edge of our seats in meetings when we discuss the mission and future direction of our churches.

I recently sat on the edge of my seat in a meeting and said, "Reaching lost people is difficult. It would be easier to reach a bunch of tithing Christians, but I am not interested in that. I am not interested in being a Christian country club around here. I moved here to start this church so we could reach the lost. I moved here to go after the hell-bent, weed-smoking, tattooed, pierced, cussing, and sexually crazed people who don't like church or preachers. That's who our church has been and will continue to be about! Do you want to know why most churches are not reaching these kinds of people? Because these kinds of people are hard to reach! These people are messy. These people rock the boat! Nonetheless, they form the focus of our mission. If you are not interested in laying your life on the line for these kinds of people, you are on the wrong team." I looked around the room. I saw conviction and even tears in almost every eye. We had a great meeting that day.

Countless times in my sixteen years of vocational ministry, I have sat up on the edge of my chair and spoken with conviction to our team. Why? Because vision fades. All of us forget that what we do echoes into eternity. We all need a reminder. I need to allow God to remind me, and then I need to remind my team with great conviction.

CULTURE

A leader's job is to define and set culture. Sam Chand said in his latest book, "Culture trumps vision."[2] I couldn't agree with him more! I am more convinced than ever before that we can have the most biblical mission statement any church has ever had, but if our team culture is toxic, we will not be successful in accomplishing the vision. The truth is, leaders set culture by design or by default. As leaders of our teams, we must set the type of team leadership and growth culture that will allow our team and our mission to be successful.

I am a big fan of ministry team values. Most new churches today not only have a mission statement but also have a list of core values their members seek to adhere to. However, I have run across very few churches or organizations that have core values that determine how their team members relate to each other. To create a healthy team culture, these cannot just be aspirational values. They must be realized values. We must actually value them!

About three years into Mountain Lake Church's existence, I walked into a team meeting one day and posed a question: "What has made our team successful? We have a great team. We have a healthy team. Why do you think that is so?" We began to write on a large piece of paper. When we finished, we had come up with seven best practices of ministry that have since defined our team culture at Mountain Lake. These days we call it "The Code." Here are our seven ministry team values:

MOUNTAIN LAKE CHURCH
MINISTRY TEAM VALUES

1. **Community: We love and do life with each other.**
   "Dear friends, since God loved us that much, we surely ought to love each other." (1 John 4:11)

2. **Honesty: We speak the truth in love.**
   "As iron sharpens iron, so a friend sharpens a friend." (Prov. 27:17)

3. **Teamwork: We work together.**
   "He makes the whole body fit together perfectly. As each part does its own special work, it helps the other parts grow, so that the whole body is healthy and growing and full of love." (Eph. 4:16)

4. **Loyalty: We protect each other.**
   "You younger men must accept the authority of the elders. And all of you, serve each other in humility, for 'God opposes the proud but favors the humble.' " (1 Pet. 5:5)

5. **Resourcefulness: We honor God with what we have.**
   "And whatever you do or say, do it as a representative of the Lord Jesus, giving thanks through him to God the Father." (Col. 3:17)

6. **Execution: We do what we say we will do.**
   "Just say a simple, 'Yes, I will,' or 'No, I won't.' Anything beyond this is from the evil one." (Matt. 5:37)

7. **Sacrifice: We're willing to pay the price.**
   "Work willingly at whatever you do, as though you were working for the Lord rather than for people." (Col. 3:23)

When Jesus got ready to change the world, he selected a team. He poured into them. He did life with them. He was constantly pulling away from the crowds to be with his team. He told them things about the kingdom of heaven he didn't tell anyone else. He allowed himself to be known by them. When everything in his own life was hitting the fan, he called them close and asked them to "watch and pray" with him (Matt. 26:41 NIV). Then Jesus released and empowered them to do ministry. He gave them authority and significant ministry to do in his stead. If Jesus valued and needed a great team, don't you think we do? Pastors, would you commit to think TEAM more often? Would you be willing to measure success more by the health, spiritual growth, and unity of your team? Success is more about the health and growth of our team than about our clever strategy and preaching.

INSIGHT

Dan Reiland, author of Amplified Leadership
and executive pastor at 12Stone Church, Lawrenceville, GA

"If we want to lead our team effectively, we must spend time with and demonstrate care for our team!" I couldn't agree more with Shawn. The team we lead must know we care, and how we show that care matters.

There are primarily two ways you can invest in the teams you lead. In these two ways you make a significant contribution that can literally be life changing. First, as Shawn talked about, you care about them. You can nurture your team in ways that let them know you value each one individually as a person. Second, you invest in their professional growth. You can make a lasting contribution to their life through world-class leadership development. The first addresses their soul; the second addresses their skill. It's the second one I'd like to briefly discuss.

I am fortunate to have been developed by the best. I'm grateful beyond measure for those who have contributed to my leadership. From Keith Drury to John Maxwell, they've changed my life, and I have no doubt that my kingdom impact would be far less without them. That is part of my passion to pass this insight on to you. Your team will be stronger and your church will reach farther because you invest in their spiritual leadership.

Leadership development is the road to empowerment, and your team will thrive when truly empowered. There is a direct correlation in the local church between control and development. In churches where development is high, control is low. Where development is low, control is high.

In churches where the team is developed, there is no need to control. Trust is high, competence is strong, and communication is clear. The team soars.

Don't make leadership development complicated. It can be as simple as this: Select the group you want to develop. Then choose a good book on leadership. Meet with the group once or twice a month to discuss the book and wrestle with these two questions. First, what are you learning? Second, how are you applying what you're learning? That's it! If you do that for a long, long time, you will be amazed at the results. Yes, you can do more. But go for consistency before you add complexity. You will be tempted to break rhythm for the tyranny of the "ministry urgent"—resist the temptation. Be ruthless in your commitment to leadership development. You and your team will be glad you did!

QUESTIONS FOR MEASUREMENT

1. Why is team building so important within the church?

2. On a scale of 1 to 10, with 1 being completely dysfunctional and 10 being utopian community, how would you rate your team? Why?

3. Which of Mountain Lake's values do you admire the most?

4. Does your staff have a set of values you hold to as a team? Why or why not?

7

PROPHECY, CRITICISM, AND SUCCESS

PAYING THE PRICE FOR MINISTRY SUCCESS

In the Old Testament, each time God wanted to do something significant with his people, he would raise up a prophet. "Surely the Sovereign LORD does nothing without revealing his plan to his servants the prophets" (Amos 3:7 NIV). In other words, God consistently chooses to work through chosen people. As we read through the Old Testament, we clearly see how prominent prophets were. Moses, Joshua, Amos, Jonah, Micah, and Isaiah were just a few of the messengers God sent to speak to and lead his people. In the New Testament too, prophecy is alive and well. John the Baptist, Peter, and John were all chosen to spread the message of God.

Even after Jesus left the earth, prophecy did not become extinct, did it? Many people continued to be used by God to lay the foundation of the early church. Peter, quoting the prophet Joel, discussed the role that prophecy would have even in the last days: " 'In the last days,' God says, 'I will pour out my Spirit upon all people. Your sons and daughters will prophesy. Your young men will see visions, and your old men will dream dreams. In those days I will pour out my Spirit even on my servants—men and women alike—and they will prophesy' " (Acts 2:17–18).

God is looking for people through whom he can speak to a lost and dying world. God is looking for people he can use to display his power and glory and to reveal his love to his children. Does that interest anyone? I know plenty of men and women who would sign on the dotted line for that assignment.

But wait. For that prophecy to be fulfilled in and through our lives, you and I are going to have to embrace the full calling that comes with the privilege of prophecy and the gift of speaking God's message. What does it require? Selflessness. For God to speak through us, we must fully submit ourselves to him. We must willingly place ourselves at his disposal to be used his way and speak his words. Ultimately, we must cast aside our own agenda, which is no small feat. Prophets have a few key characteristics.

PROPHETS GET THEIR VISION FROM GOD

God says, "I will pour out my Spirit" (Acts 2:17). This means prophets never define the vision for themselves. The verse says that God will pour out his Spirit, not that God will put his stamp of approval on our agenda. Prophets must get the vision from God. In theory, this sounds simple enough. Living it out, however, is a different story. Although almost all of us start our ministry journey with a clear understanding of the assignment God has for us, somewhere along the way we muddy the water. Losing sight of his vision, we unintentionally substitute our own vision, and the revised vision is much more about us than we would care to admit. Our visions become about what we think, what we want, what we like, how we think things ought to be done, and how our ministries ought to be structured. Many of our churches are led by preference rather than prophecy. However, if we want to be the type of prophet God uses in these last days, we have to accept that we do not invent or strategically shape the vision. This means, by the way, that we don't get our vision from a conference speaker, another church, a website, a tweet, or a blog. True prophets receive a vision only from God.

The implications of this truth are staggering. If we deny ourselves and submit all control to God, he will reveal himself to us. He will use us to speak to people who desperately need him, and he will fill us with himself. But the opposite holds true as well. If we choose to substitute our own vision for his, he won't reveal himself, he won't use us, and he won't pour out his Spirit on us. You and I have to radically alter our schedules so we can spend time taking in the vision God has for us and for our ministries. This means we must spend more unhurried, uninterrupted time with him, listening to him and reading his Word in order to glean what he wants to say to our particular ministry area, our church, our community, and our world. In these last days, God is looking for men and women who will get their vision from God, and when he finds them, he will use them.

> **Many of our churches are led by preference rather than prophecy.**

PROPHETS CHALLENGE THE STATUS QUO

My favorite biblical prophet is John the Baptist because that guy was crazy. John was not a very deep preacher. He really only had one sermon: "Repent, for the Kingdom of Heaven has come near" (Matt. 3:2 NIV). He wasn't overly creative, although he ought to score some points for the camel hair wardrobe. But maybe his message had more layers than we realize.

Of course, we get the obvious implication of his sermon: repent and turn to the coming Messiah. But let's peel back another layer. The word *repent* literally means to change the way we think. We must change the way we think before we change the way we act. At Mountain Lake Church, one of our passions is "changing the way people think about church." We have actually used that tagline in many of our publications. It is quite possible that many of us, as Christians, need to repent from—change—the way we think of the church. In order to get the most accurate picture of the mission of the church, we need to have an accurate picture of Jesus. A lot of Christians need to be challenged in terms of what it means to be a Christian. As prophets, it is our responsibility to call people to repentance, challenging the way they think about Christians and the church.

We live in a consumer-oriented world, and the me-ism mentality has certainly infiltrated the American church. So many Christians these days take something as profound as submitting to Jesus and serving him through the local church and turn it into something self-centered. The only interest most Christians have in the church these days is what it can offer them. We expect attitudes like that from those who are checking out the church for the first time, and we work hard to overcome the negative preconceived ideas they might have about the church. But here it is Christians I am talking about. My experience—and the evidence from across our nation—reveals that Christians are looking for a church that meets their needs, ministers to their kids, and offers the programs they prefer. Unless the church scratches their itch or gives them the platform or programs they want, they jump from church to church until they find one that does. Some spend their entire lives looking for the perfect church to suit them.

We must challenge the status quo. We must confront culture and be bold enough to go against the grain. When we communicate a fresh vision from God that challenges the status quo, some will disagree with us. No prophet has ever gotten 100 percent support from everyone. But take heart. Jesus couldn't even get 100 percent support from his twelve closest supporters! He had one guy who was kissing him on the cheek while stabbing him in the back! So what did we expect? Why would we think that our ministries would be different from those of every other prophet who has ever lived?

The only interest most Christians have in the church these days is what it can offer them.

If you are new to the ministry scene, allow me to enlighten you and save you some shock. If you start speaking like a prophet and challenging the status quo by changing methods or questioning intent, it won't be long until you are approached by a group that wants to "meet and talk about some things." Thus was the case with Nehemiah. "When word came to Sanballat, Tobiah, Geshem the Arab and the rest of our enemies that I had rebuilt the wall and not a gap was left in it—though up to that time I had not set the doors in the gates—Sanballat and Geshem sent me this message: 'Come, let us meet together in one of the villages on the plain of Ono.' But they were scheming to harm me" (Neh. 6:1–2 NIV). Talking is good; schemes are not.

Now let me pause here long enough to ask the obvious: Who loves confrontation? Who enjoys having enemies? Who loves having people oppose you and talk badly about you? Who enjoys having critics and being criticized? I don't enjoy any of it. Most of us would rather avoid critics and criticism at all costs, so we either fail to challenge anything or we compromise when we do.

When we got into ministry, did we really expect that we could spend the rest of our lives calling people to repentance and never be criticized? Did we really think we would never have opposition or enemies? Did we really think that we would be the one exception among all the prophets who ever lived? I'm not sure what we expected when we entered the ministry, but I do not think most of us fully embrace the call to be prophets. Being God's chosen person is not always easy. Sure, it makes for a great story, but actually living it out can be costly.

Nehemiah had this little group of people who misunderstood him and stirred up trouble, in spite of the fact that he was right in the middle of a great work of God:

> The fifth time, Sanballat's servant came with an open letter in his hand, and this is what it said:
> "There is a rumor among the surrounding nations, and Geshem tells me it is true, that you and the Jews are planning to rebel and that is why you are building the wall. According to his reports, you plan to be their king. He also reports that you have appointed prophets in Jerusalem to proclaim about you, 'Look! There is a king in Judah!'
> "You can be very sure that this report will get back to the king, so I suggest that you come and talk it over with me." (Neh. 6:5–7)

Nehemiah's story reminds us once again of several things. First of all, critics rarely oppose us overtly. Passive-aggressive criticism is pretty typical. It sometimes comes in the form of an open letter or blanket email. At times, it is even anonymous. (I never see the anonymous ones, by the way. My assistant trashes them. God's design for dealing with conflict is to address it personally and privately but not anonymously.) Some people choose to publish their dissent via Facebook or Twitter or a blog post, or they choose a more old-fashioned route and start a damaging rumor, like Nehemiah experienced. Times have changed; critics have not.

Every prophet has faced critics and naysayers, and every prophet has had to embrace criticism and loss. The tragedy is that many pastors equate a lack of criticism with success. That equation only holds true if we are talking about character. If no one can criticize your character, that certainly is success. But many of us back down from challenging the status quo in order to avoid criticism, which would by default make our character worthy of criticism. Let's not damage the cause of Christ by shrinking back from what he has called us to do. Criticism may actually be a measure of success.

Many pastors equate a lack of criticism with success.

So how do we respond to critics and criticism in our ministries? Just like Nehemiah did. First, we shouldn't spend so much time listening to our critics. We need to be like Nehemiah, who said, " 'I am carrying on a great project and cannot go down. Why should the work stop while I leave it and go down to you?' Four times they sent me the same message, and each time I gave them the same answer" (Neh. 6:3–4 NIV). In other words, "I know God has given us a call, and I am busy being obedient to that call. I don't have time to slow down and hang out with the people who are pulling in the other direction." Wow, that's permission-giving, isn't it? Most of us would tend to think that kind of response is not very godly. Nehemiah shows us otherwise. When he is summoned to meet with his critics, he basically says, "No, I don't even have time to mess with you. God has spoken. We are on a mission here, and I don't have time to slow down for the distraction of critics."

Don't misunderstand. I am not saying we should ignore people or prevent other people from speaking into our lives. I am not saying we should be jerks in ministry. I have seen that attitude lived out, and it is beneficial to no one. I am not saying we should be unteachable or uncoachable. I know some pastors who are, and their ministries are stunted. I am not saying we should avoid being critiqued. In truth, there is a big difference between a constructive critique and a criticism. A constructive critique has my best interests and the interests of the church in mind. A criticism has only the selfish interests of another person in mind. Once I determine that a criticism is serving only to reinforce a person's selfishness or sin of preference, I stop giving that person or group of people my ear. Prophets have time for constructive critiques. They don't have time for critics. Nehemiah sure didn't. We shouldn't either.

At our church I personally have two teams of people I trust to speak into my life and into my ministry at a high level: a finance team and an advisory team. These groups give me counsel and feedback and help me see what I might otherwise miss. They offer encouragement, support, and accountability. They have permission to ask probing questions about my character and my leadership. However, this group does not make the ministry or personnel decisions for our church. They only give counsel. Our pastors, having listened to their counsel, then make decisions with that counsel in mind. We have reserved the right as pastors to make the final decisions and lead the church under the Lord's leadership as he speaks to us. I really believe that in the New Testament church, the pastors are the shepherds and are, therefore, the leaders of the flock. Sheep don't lead the flock. Shepherds do.

Prophets challenge the status quo. They are bold enough to challenge our methods and thoughts, and they are smart enough to know the difference between critiques and criticism. Are you a prophet God could work in and through? Are you up to the task?

PROPHETS CONFRONT DISUNITY

I don't know anyone who enjoys confrontation. Pastors are no exception. Just like everyone else, we deal with the temptation to cover over conflict or sweep things under the rug for fear of the outcome if we speak out. Nevertheless, we must confront sin in our churches. All of us have experienced the humbling moment in which we have confronted a person's sin and called him or her to account in love. Our goal is always to restore them to spiritual health, to protect them, and to protect those affected by their actions, yet I often hear of ministry leaders who avoid confrontation when it comes to disunity in the church.

Casting doubt on the leadership of the church, stirring up dissension, or creating divisions within the body of Christ is just as sinful and damaging as an adulterous affair or any other sin that God would require us to address. More often than not, though, I watch as pastors choose to let disunity run rampant! Rather than confronting the individual or group and attempting to correct their behavior and protect the church's integrity, some of us wait it out or pretend we are unaware. Why don't we just speak the truth in love? Why won't we confront the sin? Hoping the situation will die down won't get the job done. Hoping the divisive individual won't be believed does not provide any protection for the unity of the church.

I believe that God is looking for men and women who will confront people when they attempt to derail or hijack God's vision for the church. I know we often think that if we leave a situation alone, it will go away. It is just not true. Paul said, "This false teaching is like a little yeast that spreads through the whole batch of dough!" (Gal. 5:9). A little divisiveness in our churches can cause much harm not only to the Christians among us but also to the unbelievers who are learning about God from us.

So how do we find the courage, determination, and motivation to consistently stamp out disunity in our churches? This is where our definition of success is everything. In John 17 Jesus prayed that we might be unified, and then he went a step further in his prayer for our unity. He acknowledged that a watching

117

world would know that he is in fact the Messiah based on the unity within his church. That's powerful. Clinging to that truth can give us the courage to confront disunity.

Is it possible that someone might leave your church if confronted? Could they even entice others to go with them? The answer is yes. But where in Scripture does God say to hold on to everyone? Actually, Jesus gave specific instructions for us to follow if people weren't willing to repent when confronted with their sin: "Then if he or she won't accept the church's decision, treat that person as a pagan or a corrupt tax collector" (Matt. 18:17).

That doesn't sound very Christian, does it? It sounds harsh, but it was Christ who told us to operate this way. Jesus expects us to confront sin and disunity, and he expects us to protect his church. We are his undershepherds, after all. He has tasked us with shielding his flock from potential harm. Comments and agendas that threaten the unity of our churches can most definitely harm his flock. All of the New Testament affirms that from God's perspective, success is not a large church or a small church or a traditional church or a contemporary church. Success is a unified church, not a conflict-free church. We cannot keep the church unified by shying away from conflict. We keep the church unified by resolving it. Jesus never said we would be different because we wouldn't have conflict in the church. He said we would be different by the way we resolved it.

Success is a unified church, not a conflict-free church.

PROPHETS ENDURE CRITICISM AND LOSS

I know what some of you are thinking: "Shawn, that's easy for you to say. You don't have the same baggage and challenges that we do. You don't have powerful people in your church opposed to you or criticizing you." Are you kidding me? Since we started Mountain Lake, I've taken on challenges and faced the criticism of countless individuals and groups. Friends—close friends—have stabbed me in the back, turned on me, and falsely accused me.

My favorite accusation against me was that I started our church "for the money." The accusation actually hurt a lot. Someone had doubted my integrity and character and intentions, and the personal attacks always sting the worst. Suffice it to say, I have been accused of much of which I am not guilty. I am not the only one. Jeremiah was accused of insanity. Nehemiah was accused of being obsessive. Joel was accused of being negative. Jesus was accused of blasphemy. Peter was accused of heresy. Paul was accused of being greedy. Countless more pastors and ministry leaders have faced hurtful accusations. We are not alone.

It is not easy to keep moving forward in the face of criticism, accusations, and rumors. When the criticism flies, we are going to be tempted to give up the great work God has called us to. We simply cannot! If criticism distracts us from God's redemptive mission, we'll never finish our assignment, and we certainly won't achieve success.

One of the reasons Churchplanters.com is dedicated to supporting coaching relationships and coaching networks is because so often we just need to gain perspective from an outside voice assuring us that our experience is normal, even expected. Coaching relationships more often than not help all of us to stay the course in difficult times. Many of the emails and phones calls I get from pastors around the world begin with, "Shawn, I've got this guy . . ." or "I've got this group. . . ." Most of the time, pastors actually know deep down what they should do. All they need is someone to say: "Make the call. Have the conversation. Deal with the issue. Confront the person." At Churchplanters.com, we call that "giving pastors permission"—permission to speak up, permission to draw a line in the sand, permission to do what everyone already knows needs to be done.

I take great comfort in the long list of prophets who have gone before me and have faced greater criticism and attack than I have. I also take great encouragement that those who were criticized were also being used mightily by God. The two are directly related. The center of God's will is often a dangerous place to be. The only way we can escape criticism is to say nothing, do nothing, and be nothing. I guarantee that if you stop speaking for God, become a people-pleaser, and stop trying to reach out to a lost and dying world, you will cease to be criticized. You will no longer be a target. You will also be of little use to God. The moment you start speaking for God, challenging people's thinking, and focusing your church on being a hospital for sinners, watch out! You will have a bull's-eye on your chest. Criticism is never far from the leader's life. Embrace it. It comes with the territory. It's nothing new. The early church dealt with it from the very beginning. "But as the believers rapidly multiplied, there were rumblings of discontent" (Acts 6:1).

Have you ever read such an encouraging word? If Peter, James, and John faced rumblings, we will too. Bill Hybels has said, "Somewhere along the way, I conceded the point that the more influence you carry, the bigger target you wear."[1] I have certainly found that to be true. God is looking for prophets on whom he can pour out his Spirit—prophets who recognize that criticism comes with the call to be a prophet. We will be accused. People are going to get upset. We're going to have to release people from our ministry and care. People are going to leave. We are going to lose followers along the way. We might even lose a few "friends." Jesus did. Loss will bring hurt, loneliness, and discouragement our way. Nevertheless, God is looking for men and women who will stand up under the strain of criticism and even loss.

There are three things every pastor needs to know:

1. Pastoring is hard.
2. Pastoring is very hard.
3. Pastoring is the hardest thing you could do with your life.

Encouraged? I only share this message because I meet too many people who want the privilege of being a pastor without paying the price of being a prophet. Prophets endure criticism and loss. We had better count the cost!

PROPHETS LIVE TO PLEASE THE RIGHT AUDIENCE

Prophets have always had to make a decision. Moses and Jesus both made their decision in the desert. Jonah made his in the belly of a whale. Paul made his on the road to Damascus. What decision? The decision to live for the right audience. Two thousand years later, we as pastors take our stages, platforms, and pulpits every weekend, and we make an often unconscious, inadvertent choice: Which audience will I seek to please? Every prophet who has ever lived has felt the same tension and faced the same choice. C. H. Spurgeon said, "You are not sent of God to court smiles but to win souls."[2] Paul said, "Obviously, I'm not trying to win the approval of people, but of God. If pleasing people were my goal, I would not be Christ's servant" (Gal. 1:10). Prophets—people chosen by God to speak on his behalf—must daily choose whom they will seek to please.

Writing this book has been a humbling exercise for me. I have really put myself out there by confessing personal opinions and several areas of failure. I realize that as people read this book I will be criticized, critiqued, and even judged. I am tempted to care far too much what you think about this book, what you think about me, and what you think about my opinions. I care what you think because I want you to like me and to be impressed by my knowledge and skill. My temptation is to write a book that will primarily be witty and funny and one you will enjoy.

121

As I write these pages, however, God reminds me that I cannot make that my goal.

God has used his Word to show me the difference between a prophet he chooses to use and a false prophet. Here it is: false prophets tell people what they want to hear. They seek to please the people around them rather than living at the disposal of almighty God. They preach their own agenda at the expense of God's mission. God reminds me consistently that I cannot do that. Pleasing the wrong audience would negate my ministry and disqualify me from hearing the words I crave at the end of my journey: "Well done, thou good and faithful servant." I don't want to spend my whole life in ministry only to get to heaven and realize I have served the wrong master. God anointed and appointed me to speak for him. He has spoken to me and given me his vision for his church. What a privilege and honor! God help me if I stray from his calling.

I am determined. I will not go away, get off track, quit, or even be quiet until God says and does everything he wants to in and through me. I choose to please only one person. I live to please one audience. My Lord and Savior Jesus Christ didn't back down from critics, naysayers, or even people who wanted to kill him. I am resolved to be his prophet.

What about you? God is looking for people who will answer the call to become his prophets. The price is high. In fact, it could cost us everything. But if we choose to stand up and answer the call in spite of the sacrifice and remain committed to his vision, the reward will be worth it.

INSIGHT

Chris Seay, author of A Place at the Table
and pastor of Ecclesia, Houston, TX

Shawn simultaneously calls us to embrace the biblical role of a prophet, which is too often misunderstood, and warns us that doing so will create chaos, pain, and loss. It's about time someone told the whole truth on this subject. Leading a church well inevitably leads to pain, criticism, accusations, and worse. But that should not deter us from seeking to speak for God to his people. God is not merely searching for effective leaders; he needs us to step forward and passionately call people to live into his vision. My grandfather (a pastor for sixty years) told me many times as I considered my vocation, "If you can do anything else, do it. But if you have no other choice and God has made it clear to you, get ready for a long, hard, and beautifully painful road."

Walter Brueggemann says that a prophet uses his words to simultaneously paint a picture of the world as it is and as it should be. This creates tension, but without tension we will not see a vision of the kingdom and move toward it. Shawn reminds us that this tension has been around since the church began. But I do believe technology has created an accessibility unique to our day. Discontent is now easily channeled into emails and blog posts hastily written in anger. I have had to find ways to shake off painful words that are hard to forget. Exercise, prayer, and encouragement from faithful friends have been invaluable in the wake of hurtful words.

QUESTIONS FOR MEASUREMENT

1. Do you agree with Shawn's assessment that every pastor is a prophet? Why or why not?

2. What is the most difficult part of being a prophet? Why?

3. Is there a specific courageous conversation you need to have or decision you need to make that God brought to mind as you read this chapter? If so, what do you need to do?

4. How does this chapter encourage you?

8

FEEL LIKE
QUITTING?

MAYBE YOU SHOULD . . . MAYBE YOU SHOULDN'T

Have you ever been tempted to quit? To stop preaching? To step down from leadership? To walk away from the difficulties, the emotional strain, the financial burdens, the isolation, and the managerial demands of leadership? If you have, you are not alone. Jesus was tempted to quit. Take a closer look at the three temptations of Christ in Matthew 4, and you'll see the temptation to quit woven throughout the story. Satan enticed Jesus to question God, question himself, and question his calling, and Satan does the same to us. He knows that if we doubt our God or our calling, we're likely to throw in the towel. The scenario goes something like this: tithes are in the tank, you feel inadequate as a preacher, a staff member quits, and then a major church conflict erupts. Isn't that when you are tempted to walk away? In times like that, you doubt God, you doubt his ability to use you, and it just seems easier to pack it in. It is sometimes an unspoken temptation, but it is not uncommon.

I meet many pastors and ministry leaders every year who struggle with the temptation to quit. We can't verbalize our struggle in our church, however. After all, what would our church members think? Or the staff we lead? They would surely never follow someone so emotionally unstable, right? At least that's what we tell ourselves. So we struggle in silence, often feeling there's no way out.

One national ministry leader and frequent conference speaker told me he had challenged pastors at a recent conference to think about why they remain in vocational ministry. He told them that if they were just hanging on to vocational ministry for the financial security it provided, they should email him, and he would help get them out of ministry and secure them other employment. He had several emails in his inbox before he got home! As it turns out, not only do many of us deal with the temptation to quit, but some of us are actively searching for a way out. Frankly, I have never met a ministry leader who didn't deal with the temptation to quit at some point, and many are succumbing to the temptation.

What would you do if you quit vocational ministry today? Think about it. If I were to quit, I would go back into the real estate business. Do you ever think about it? If so, you've just revealed the fact that you've been tempted to quit! Entertaining thoughts of another life is a certain indication that all is not well in paradise. I'm not pointing a finger. I'm with you. I'm tempted to quit about every seven days. The temptation is not our problem. Our response to the temptation is. The temptation to quit is not a sin. Quitting is!

THE ROLLER-COASTER RIDE

Ministry includes the highest of highs and the lowest of lows. On the one hand, we celebrate life's changes and spiritual wins. On the other, we struggle with feelings of discouragement and defeat. One day we're riding high after a good turnout for a volunteer meeting. The next day we're discouraged when some of those volunteers don't show up for service. One day we ride a tidal wave of fun after a huge baptism service. The next day we are knocked down as we face criticism from a not-so-well-meaning member of the community. The roller-coaster ride of ministry can leave us out of breath and ready to bail.

Jesus understands the temptation. He's ridden the same ride. Before Jesus entered the desert to be tempted, he had been baptized by John the Baptist. As he came up out of the water, surrounded by a crowd of witnesses, Jesus heard his Father say, "This is my Son, whom I love; with him I am well pleased" (Matt. 3:17 NIV). No greater compliment could be paid to a ministry servant. The crowd was cheering him on. His Father was building him up.

Crowds and compliments help form the biggest ministry highs. When the crowds are marching with us and the pats on the back are plentiful, the ride is fun, satisfying, and fulfilling. But coasters always have dips, don't they? When God blesses our ministry and the crowds and the compliments soar, Satan is right there, trying to discourage and defeat us.

Probably one of the biggest mistakes I made when entering ministry was overlooking spiritual warfare. I didn't connect the dots. I didn't realize that those people, that email, that phone call, that group of people, that fight with my wife, or that sickness was a temptation to become discouraged and feel defeated. I failed to recognize those types of circumstances as a distraction to my mission causing me to take my eyes off the prize. Overwhelming emotional demands would sometimes leave me questioning my desire to continue. Becoming more aware of Satan's schemes has helped me deal with the temptation to quit. When great things are happening in my ministry, I have learned,

I need to prepare for the coming desert experience and for the temptation to get discouraged and quit.

When my wife and I started Mountain Lake Church, we were faced with disappointment, defeat, and discouragement from the very start. We were even tempted to quit after our first core group meeting! Let me give you some perspective. When Tricia and I moved to Cumming, a suburb of Atlanta, we didn't know anyone in our community. Our church was what is referred to as a "parachute plant." We dropped in on a community that was entirely new to us. Step one was simply making friends with our neighbors. At first we didn't even want anyone to know we worked for a church. Walls go up immediately, if you know what I mean. We just wanted to make friends with unchurched people. So for the first two months in our new community, we tried to keep our profession on the down low, and we simply got to know people in our neighborhood and community.

Finally, the night came when we would pull back the blinds and reveal our intentions. We hosted a barbecue at our house, and eighteen of our unchurched friends and neighbors showed up. At the end of the night, I stood up and said, "Guys, most of you don't know what I do for a living. I'm actually a pastor, and Tricia and I moved here to start a new church in this community. We are launching this new church in our home next Wednesday at 6:30. There won't be any preaching. We'll just eat together, get to know each other, and discuss the Bible a little bit. I would love for you to consider coming back." Shockingly, on the way out that night, every single one of our eighteen friends told us they would be back to check it out. Ministry high.

One week later, we cleaned, cooked, and prepared for the first core group meeting of Mountain Lake Church. Never has a living room/house of God been so prepared. We put out the spread of food. We lit candles to give it a homey feeling. We had extra Bibles on hand. Cool tunes were playing. I had prepared a great study from the book of Acts on relationships. We prayed together. This was going to be great. Finally, 6:30 came. Then 7:00 came. Then 7:30 came. No people came. Not one person ever showed up that night. Ministry low.

We had zero guests at our first worship service. You can't start off worse than that. Sure, it's funny now. It wasn't funny then. I literally curled up in the fetal position in bed, and I silently cried myself to sleep. Tricia tried to comfort me, but I was sure she was thinking, "What has this idiot gotten us into?" Believe me, I was wondering the exact same thing.

That experience was just the first of many times when my expectations and reality did not meet. It was the first of many days when I would feel defeated and discouraged. I have certainly enjoyed many high days in ministry, but I have experienced some low ones too. It comes with the calling. Ministry can be a roller coaster of emotions.

> We determined that whether we served two or two thousand, we would not give up.

The next morning, Tricia and I began to encourage one another. We agreed that discouragement would come, but we would not give in to feelings of defeat. We determined that whether we served two or two thousand, we would not give up. We resolved in our hearts and minds that we would not quit until God did everything he wanted to do in and through us at Mountain Lake. We got down on our knees and prayed, and then we dusted ourselves off and got back in the saddle. We've been doing that every week since.

Behind every low time a ministry high is looming. I refuse to give in to the temptation to quit during the low times, because I refuse to make life-altering decisions in the middle of bad circumstances. I refuse to ride the roller coaster of ministry and try to bail out when it gets scary. I choose, instead, to follow the example of Jesus and endure. If God has a change in mind for me, I trust that he will make it evident in more ways than just my circumstances.

I would like to say that the next week, all eighteen of our friends showed up for our second core group meeting, but actually only two of them showed up at our home. The next week we rocked the living room with four. One man and wife became believers in the following weeks, and all four continue to be active members of our church to this day. Ministry high.

It's a tragedy that some of us quit just before the next ministry high lifts our spirits. Remember Paul's admonition? "Let us not become weary in doing good, for *at the proper time* we will reap a harvest if we do not give up" (Gal. 6:9 NIV, emphasis added).

> **Most pastors quit just before the harvest.**

Maybe we should carve those words onto our office doors so we'll be encouraged to endure when we feel like slamming that door and walking out. If you are experiencing a low today, hold on to the promise that if you will be faithful to your calling, a high is coming at the proper time. Most pastors quit just before the harvest.

Jesus experienced highs and lows. So will we. That's not a bad thing, but the ups and downs absolutely increase our vulnerability to the temptation to quit. Follow our leader's example to determine in your heart and mind that you will not allow the roller coaster of ministry to get the best of you.

REFUSING TO REST

After fasting for forty days, Jesus was tired and weak. Fatigue set in just before Satan came along to tempt him. In an emotionally and physically weakened state, we are undoubtedly more vulnerable to temptation. If we have walked through the desert for a while or have weathered a time of attacks and whispers by the enemy, we *will* be tempted to quit. So what should we do? Rest.

That's a challenge, isn't it? Few people rest well. We live in a society that doesn't know how to rest. Instead, our culture lives in perpetual motion with constant communication and maximized agendas. Emails and cell phones keep us moving at a frantic pace even from our living rooms, and fear of falling behind robs many of us of the rest we desperately need.

Yet we know that fatigue makes us weaker against temptation. So if refusing to rest makes us more vulnerable to quitting, yet we continue to squeeze every second out of every day, we must address the real issue of our hearts. Do you trust God enough to take him at his word when he says that resting every six days is best for you? Are you willing to live your life his way, or will you continue to live it your way? When you get right down to it, resting is a faith issue. I'm not advocating a form of legalism that requires us all to hibernate one day each week, but I am suggesting that disobeying God's command will eventually cost each of us.

I have fought for a day off. I haven't had to fight my church or my advisory team. I've had to fight myself, my mind that won't shut down, my urge to return a few emails, and my desire to work ahead. With great discipline, I choose to rest. Ironic, isn't it? I work hard to rest.

Practically speaking, I take Mondays off. I have chosen that day for a couple of reasons. Number one: more often than any other day, it can be one of those "ministry low" days. I might not feel as if I preached well enough on Sunday, attendance may or may not have met my expectation, and that's when the negative phone calls hit the voice mail or the negative emails hit the inbox. Why not avoid that by taking Monday off? Number two: Monday is an easier day to rest for me because everything can be put off on Monday! It is the least urgent day of the week when it comes to preaching. On each following day, the next message I'm preparing requires more attention, and I feel the urgency building for the coming weekend.

Which day to take off each week is inconsequential. The key is that we value rest in our lives. Choose a work-rest rhythm that works for you and your family.

I know that when pastors are tired, they are more vulnerable to temptation. So when our church launched Saturday night services a few years ago, we set into place a "preservation plan" to keep our team refreshed in the midst of a demanding weekend schedule. The plan not only outlined how much vacation time each pastor has but also highlighted the fact that each pastor is required to take it all! We gave more vacation, more days off, and more comp days. We also became stricter about our pastors keeping realistic office hours and not being at the office on their day off. Our pastors are not expected to be out more than two nights per week for ministry-related activities. Sure, there are exceptions, but if this value is violated on a consistent basis, I address it. I feel a mandate from God to help preserve the team he has given me and to help them overcome the temptation to quit in response to fatigue.

Just as I hold my team accountable to rest, I require the same of myself. I am almost never out more than two nights per week, and I've asked my assistant to help me guard my time. I have also asked my wife to hold me accountable, and she is more than willing. She helps preserve me. I currently take about six weeks of vacation each year. Two of these weeks are back-to-back weeks in the summer. That second week is always amazing, because I have already had an entire week to shut down my crazy mind and to begin to think and move at a different pace. The second week recharges my batteries like no other experience during the year. Building rest into my life also means I don't teach at my church every weekend. Teaching too much drains my energy, so I try not to teach more than 70 percent of the time.

Our church has both Saturday and Sunday services. Over the whole weekend, there's not a full day of rest for me as a pastor. It is a lot of work. But once I make it home after church, I turn off my phone for a while and catch a nap on the couch. Literal physical rest does wonders. Mondays my batteries charge fully, and then I re-engage! My spirit recharges as my body does, and I'm much better mentally equipped to tackle life.

These are just a few of the things I do to keep myself rested and recharged. I have learned the hard way that if I don't rest, I will be more vulnerable to the temptation to quit in the days to come. You will too. After seventeen years of vocational ministry, I am finally learning how to rest. Do you trust God enough to live life his way and rest consistently? What's your plan?

DESERT EXPERIENCES

Where was Jesus when he was facing his three great temptations? Alone in the desert. We all have desert experiences.

Moses did. David did. Elijah did. Job did. Jonah did. Isaiah did. John did. Paul did. Jesus did.

Every person who has ever been used by God has been tempted during a desert experience. The question is not whether we will face desert experiences in our lives. The question is whether we'll go through the desert alone. I don't know of any greater way to be tempted to quit than to walk alone into the desert to face trials and burdens by ourselves. If we want to put ourselves in the exact same position as Jesus here and walk into the desert alone, we can try. We need to keep in mind that our relationship with God isn't quite as strong as Jesus's. We're not part of the Trinity. We're not a spiritual Superman or even a Clark Kent. What makes us most vulnerable to the temptation to quit is living on a spiritual island. Even Jesus wanted replenishing relationships in his life.

When I am feeling discouraged and defeated, everything within me urges me to withdraw from the people around me, but I want to tell you that the fact that Satan is tempting you just reveals that God has big plans for you. That was the case for Jesus. Satan only tries to get people to quit when they are a threat to him and his destructive plans. So what do you do? Battle his twisted lies of deceit with the truth of God's Word. Consume God's Word. Read the Psalms. Read Joshua. The primary lesson from Jesus's temptation to quit was that we should never quit, especially when we're in the desert.

ARE YOU CALLED?

There is another reason you might be tempted to quit. You might be thinking about quitting because you need to quit. It's entirely possible that you've run ahead of God to become a pastor or a ministry leader. Wild ambition has landed many people in a place God never called them to be. The idea or vision looked so intriguing that some have jumped before receiving a clear calling from God. I must caution you that if you are working out of your own flesh and power without a clear calling from the Lord, the temptation to quit will always be present. Why? Because you are working outside of his will.

> **When you are convinced of your direction, you won't quit when the low times roll in.**

Because clarity of calling is so critical to our success, I ask people who are contemplating the ministry if they know that God has called them. If they can't answer me very quickly and with confidence, then I tell them not to move forward. What happens when a pastor or ministry leader is unsure and the journey gets difficult?

Do you know what God has called *you* to do? Are you sure of it? If not, be still before God and ask him to begin speaking loudly to you. When he reveals what you are to do, do it. Stop whatever you've been doing, turn around, and follow him in the new direction he is leading you toward. You won't know everything you're supposed to do. You will just know you're called to do it. There may be uncertainty, but things will become clearer. And when you are convinced of your direction, you won't quit when the low times roll in.

If you are currently in vocational ministry and aren't absolutely positive that God has called you into it, do yourself and the church a favor and quit. Resign. Get out now. It's only a matter of time before you quit anyway. Here's what Jesus said:

> A hired hand will run when he sees a wolf coming. He will abandon the sheep because they don't belong to him and he isn't their shepherd. And so the wolf attacks them and scatters the flock. The hired hand runs away because he's working only for the money and doesn't really care about the sheep. (John 10:12–13)

You must be more than a hired hand. You must be called by God to be a shepherd, or you will run away when times get tough.

In contrast, God's desire for those of us who are certain of the ministry we lead could be stated no better than this: "Therefore, my dear brothers and sisters, stand firm. Let nothing move you. Always give yourselves fully to the work of the Lord, because you know that your labor in the Lord is not in vain" (1 Cor. 15:58 NIV).

INSIGHT

Greg Surratt, founding pastor of Seacoast Church in Mt. Pleasant, SC, and a founding board member of the Association of Related Churches (ARC)

Shawn writes, "The primary lesson from Jesus's temptation to quit was that we should never quit, especially when we're in the desert." Boy, do I know what that is like!

One of the most discouraging moments in my life and in the life of our church, Seacoast, took place several years ago. The church had grown far beyond our expectations, and we needed to expand our building. As we planned and moved forward, things seemed to be falling into place. Then, suddenly, everything fell apart. A group of locals had joined forces to oppose growth in the town, and Seacoast was their primary target. Since it also happened to be an election year, things got pretty political.

In the end, not only were our plans not approved, but zoning rules and other restrictions were put in place that would make it even more difficult for us to expand at a later date. Talk about discouragement.

I drove back to my office, closed the door, turned off the lights, and turned on some country music. Country music is helpful when I'm feeling discouraged—in country songs, everyone loses something, whether it's a dog, truck, or wife.

How could this have happened? I asked myself. We were so sure that we were following God. Now the only thing we could be sure of was tomorrow's newspaper headline: "Megachurch Loses." How humiliating. How discouraging. I had no idea where to go from there. Fortunately, God did. It's real tough to surprise someone who is omniscient.

A few hours later, I came to my senses as I remembered God's promise in Romans 8:28 that God will cause everything to work together for good for those who love him. Well, I knew we loved God, and I knew he had something in store for our church. I knew God was working on a solution before we even knew there was a problem. He had a plan.

With one door closed, we were forced to look at alternative solutions to our growing pains. We were forced to be innovative. The truth is, innovation is just desperation in a prettier package. Our desperation drove us to look at new ways of doing church.

The solution we eventually settled on would later become known as multisite, or one church worshiping in multiple locations. As of this writing, our church has thirty-three unique worship experiences each weekend in thirteen separate locations. I know I never would have thought that one up on my own.

A few years after that discouraging night at the town council, I ran into a man who had been one of the chief opponents of our planned expansion. As he reached out to enthusiastically shake my hand, he told me that he was proud of our church and of the innovative ways we had expanded. He left me with one final thought: "Don't you think we played some small part in the success and growth of your church?"

The truth is, he was right. Without losing that town council vote, without that discouraging night, we never would have pushed beyond the box of a single location. What was thought of as our biggest failure, God used as our greatest blessing to the body of Christ.

What discouragements are you facing? What if, instead of seeing them as defeats, you saw them as God redirecting you toward something even better?

QUESTIONS FOR MEASUREMENT

1. Think about a time when you were tempted to quit. What were the circumstances that led to this?

2. When was the last time you felt like you were living in the sweet spot of your calling? What led to this feeling?

3. How can we help each other as pastors when we're tempted to quit?

PART 3

A NEW SET OF METRICS

9

MEASURING
WHAT MATTERS

CROWDS OR CONVERSIONS?

As disciples of Jesus, our primary task is to become more like him. As pastors and ministry leaders, our primary task is to teach others to become more like him. By taking a closer look at who Jesus spent time with and how he attracted people to himself, we will learn how to best lead people to God and how to effectively love them. We will also gain a clear understanding of how Jesus measured his success.

Jesus really didn't pick any religious people for his movement. He didn't pick people who were known for their super-spiritual qualities, natural talent, or wealth. His top picks might not even meet the qualifications list for many of the volunteer teams or missions groups in our modern churches. Instead, Jesus chose to focus on, pour his energy into, and entrust his mission to the *un*qualified, not the qualified.

WHO ARE WE REACHING?

Who were the types of people Jesus picked to make disciples? People like Levi. Levi is representative of the type of people who were closest to Jesus when he walked the earth: the disreputable or troubled. Levi probably made people uncomfortable when he walked into the room. Conversations stopped, if you know what I mean. Yet this is someone Jesus chose to spend time with and to disciple. Why? "When Jesus heard this, he told them, 'Healthy people don't need a doctor—sick people do. I have come to call not those who think they are righteous, but those who know they are sinners'" (Mark 2:17).

> **While we are busy making church cool and relevant, are we also making it a hospital for sinners?**

If we are to follow the example of Jesus in every way, why are most of the discipleship efforts in churches across America focused on religious people, or at least people who have been Christians their whole lives? Why does the majority of our programming relate only to Christians? Is the church as a whole guilty of being focused on itself rather than seeking to meet the needs of the spiritually sick? While so much fuss is made about fast-growing churches, is anyone wondering how much of that growth is actual conversion growth? While we are busy making church cool and relevant, are we also making it a hospital for sinners? Years ago, a friend of mine once joked that the churches in his town didn't grow; they simply swapped sheep. In years of ministry since, I have certainly seen that dynamic in play, even with some of the fastest-growing churches in America.

To be honest, most churches tend to cater to the churched crowd. Deep preaching, combined with discipleship programs and engaging environments for all ages, is the cry of the day for many. Don't get me wrong. Discipling Christians is important.

Elevating our faith and deepening our understanding and knowledge of God are crucial elements of the healthy Christian's life,
and there is no better place to deepen or grow than in God's
house. But if we only cater to the church crowd, we have a
problem. If that happens, we have ignored the example of Jesus
and we are not modeling his ministry. But generally speaking,
many of our churches are designed to meet the needs of the
people who already know God and ignore the needs of those
who are far from him.

This is the reason I planted Mountain Lake. I wanted to create a safe place where I could welcome my unchurched friends,
a place where they would be accepted as they were and allowed
some time to get to know God before being challenged to change.
At Mountain Lake, we reach out to people with little or no religious background and those with messy lives. Our goal is to lead
them to Jesus, watch their lives change in response to him, and
then prepare them to reach more people in similar situations.

We have baptized 50 percent of our current congregation's
weekly attendance. Because of the types of people we are reaching, our per capita financial giving to God is roughly half that
of a traditional established church, but that number has grown
annually by an average of one dollar per person per year since the
church started. That's statistical proof of growth in our mission.
Mountain Lake's best disciples and leaders are often formerly
messed-up people with messed-up families living messed-up
lives. Most of our small group leaders and volunteer team leaders
have never led anything in a church before serving here. Measurements like these mark our ministry metrics (and success)
more than any other. Success is reaching the spiritually sick.

The discipleship issue has many implications for how we
measure success for pastors. Do you realize that your church or
my church could be on the "100 Fastest-Growing Churches in
America" list, be viewed as successful in the eyes of everyone in
the world, but still be unsuccessful in God's eyes? Once again,

God's perspective and ours might not be on the same page. From God's perspective, who our church is reaching is far more important than how many we are reaching. If our church is growing primarily by swapping sheep or at another church's expense, we are simply not impressing Jesus or accomplishing his mission. If we are not reaching unchurched people and seeing them come to know Jesus Christ, go public with their faith, and grow in faith, we are not successful in his eyes, no matter what everyone else thinks.

THE NUMBER NO ONE TALKS ABOUT: CONVERSION GROWTH

Often when I overhear pastors talk to each other, they might describe their church in terms of musical style, teaching style, and dress style, and of course, as we've already discussed, they might say, "We're running about X number on the weekends." For them, information like that defines who their church is and what it is about. Certainly our worship style and worship attendance tell us something about a church, but they do not and should not tell the whole story!

The number that not so many churches seem to be talking about is the number of baptisms proportionate to a church's worship attendance. How much life change and spiritual fruit are we actually bearing? How many people are going public with their faith through baptism? How many people are being saved? While I am certainly pleased with the numerical growth my church has experienced since we began, that's not the most important number in our church story. The number that best reflects the testimony of God's work through Mountain Lake Church is the number of people who have laid their lives at the feet of Jesus. Over 1,500 people have now gone public with their faith in Jesus through baptism since our church began. Seventy percent of those were over the age of eighteen when they did so! Sure, I am happy to see a full auditorium when I preach each weekend, but the joy of my heart—what I count as success—is eternal fruit. Filling our auditoriums is good; filling heaven is better.

As pastors and ministry leaders, let's be careful how we measure success. If a church is averaging one hundred people on Sundays and has baptized twenty in the past year, then 20 percent of the attendance has come through conversion growth. That's incredible! At Mountain Lake, we have a goal of baptizing 15 to 20 percent of our attendance every year. We don't hit it every year, but we are holding ourselves accountable to measuring what matters and seeing unchurched people come to faith in Jesus. Why do baptisms matter to us? Baptisms represent people who have decided to submit their lives to Jesus. Our mission is to take the gospel to people and allow Jesus to change the eternal destinies of the people in our care. Growing our church through Christian consumerism isn't our goal. Seeing people come to Jesus is.

> **Filling our auditoriums is good; filling heaven is better.**

We simply cannot get caught up in measuring our ministries by our music, programs, services, campuses, and attendance. If our church is not reaching large numbers of unchurched people proportionate to the number of people who are coming, we are not being obedient to the Great Commission. We are not successful just because our congregation is large or our ministry is cutting-edge. The church does not exist just to gather Christians! Christian community that is not reaching unchurched people is not Christian community; it's consumerism.

DISCIPLESHIP GROWTH

I just don't know how Jesus ever made disciples without Christian bookstores or bound Bible studies by well-known authors, but he did. Here's what I think: if one more Bible study program was going to change the world, it would have already happened. When Jesus walked the earth, he had no printing press or three-ring binders, but he made great disciples! How? " 'Come, follow me,' Jesus said, 'and I will send you out to fish for people'" (Mark 1:17 NIV).

His disciple-making efforts were based on a relational process! As Jesus sought to make disciples, he focused more on a process than on a program. That's why I want to suggest to you that what we need is not the latest fad Bible study or program. What we need is a process built on relational connection that moves people from point A to point B, from skeptic to believer, from complacent to inspired. That's not how most of us are seeking to disciple people, is it? If you don't believe it, go get one of your worship guides and open it. Quite often, we would have to admit, it's full of programs and activities that aren't really producing spiritual fruit in people's lives. Typically we will offer these programs for a while, tire of them, and then trash them in order to unveil the new discipleship flavor of the month or year.

Our spiritual formation pastor was once at a pastors' roundtable and was asked by one of the attending pastors how we get such a large percentage of people in small groups at Mountain Lake. His answer? We don't have a perfect plan, but then again we are not looking for the perfect plan. We seek to identify our weak spots and find ways to improve our processes each year. We believe life change happens in the context of intimate groups of people who journey through life together, so we consistently teach the importance of small group community to the people of our church, and we keep the assimilation process simple. We have never chased the latest, greatest fad to make disciples, and we try to keep all other programming to a minimum. The pastor responded by saying, "Listening to you guys, it sounds like the key for you is consistency." Bull's-eye.

No discipleship plan is perfect, but we do need to have a plan that is built on relationships and then stick to it. Plan the work, then work the plan. Consistency works! I'm amazed at all the stuff we don't do at our church. We don't have vacation Bible school. We don't offer midweek children's or student activities. We don't have a family life center or an athletic league. We don't even purchase Bible study materials each year. Neither did Jesus, by the way. How did he disciple people? He developed people. He mentored through relationship.

FRUIT, NOT MEAT

Jesus was a brilliant teacher. He said more in two paragraphs than any of us could hope to preach in a lifetime. And, once again, his focus was different than what ours tends to be. Jesus focused more on life application than on Bible exposition. He focused more on doing than knowing. To be sure, you can't do until you know, but Jesus challenged his disciples to put their head knowledge to work. He focused less on preaching and more on sending. He focused more on living the Scriptures than on studying the Scriptures. If you want to talk about some abused, misused phrases in Western Christianity, let's talk about "going deeper" and needing "more meat." If we would take our cues from Jesus, we would stop trying to spiritually feed everybody the mysteries of the Bible and start teaching them to apply what they already know. Jesus focused on fruit, not meat. He focused on living out faith in action, not soaking up devotional thoughts. Some of the most vibrant Christians in our church have not been Christians all that long and don't know everything about the Bible, but they love and serve extravagantly. To me, that's as deep and spiritually mature as it gets.

"Now that you know these things, you will be blessed if you do them" (John 13:17 NIV). Most Christians are already educated far beyond their obedience. We don't need to help people discover some new truth that they have never heard before in order to make disciples. What we need to do is start holding people accountable to applying what they already know. *That's* deep! Jesus knew in his day that everybody was looking for some "new" truth, so he played off that expectation when he said, "So now I am giving you a new command-ment: Love each other. Just as I

> **Most Christians are already educated far beyond their obedience.**

have loved you, you should love each other. Your love for one another will prove to the world that you are my disciples" (John 13:34–35).

Jesus's greatest command to his followers was to love God and to love one another, yet many of our churches are full of apathetic Christians who struggle to get along with other people. And what about his commands to tithe and rest and serve? So many of our brothers and sisters in Christ fail to honor God with their resources, refuse to honor the Sabbath, and live a self-centered lifestyle. We know what Jesus wants us to do. We just don't do it. If we applied what we already know to do, the body of Christ would look much different, as would the world.

Larry Osborne, in his book *Sticky Church*, laid out a very simple plan for creating disciples. Here it is:

1. "Velcro" people to God's Word by teaching them to feed themselves from it.
2. "Velcro" people to each other.[1]

Larry's church, North Coast Church in San Diego, promotes a very simple plan to disciple people. They believe that if we follow this simple plan, people will grow in their relationship with God.

Somehow understanding this dynamic from early on, our church chose to focus our disciple-making process on application, not information—on fruit, not meat! Do we get pushback at our church from people because of our focus? Yes. Do we have people who don't stay at our church because we don't offer lots of programs? Yes. Do we have people leave because we're not "deep enough" for them? Yes. We just don't care about that. We are not going to appeal to that mentality. We *are* all about anything that will cause people to take action steps in living out the Christian life.

Do you want to know what deep is? Loving God. Loving people. Following Jesus.

LEADERS, NOT CROWDS

Jesus obviously spent time with big crowds, but a more careful look at the Gospels reveals the full story. Jesus taught the crowds about the kingdom and revealed his love for them, but he also consistently pulled away from the crowds to spend more time with the twelve specific leaders he had chosen. Even his method of teaching reveals his focus on leaders: "In his public ministry he never taught without using parables; but afterward, when he was alone with his disciples, he explained everything to them" (Mark 4:34).

Jesus taught the crowds, but he invested in leaders. In contrast to Jesus's focus, most of us tend to focus all our ministry efforts on the weekend crowds by creating great worship services. One famous pastor has often said, "It's all about the weekend, stupid." For years I believed it too. I don't believe it anymore.

At our church these days, our leaders are held accountable for meeting with the leaders under their care at least once every thirty days for discipleship and ministry skill enhancement. We believe that everything in our church rises and falls on leadership. I personally meet monthly with two of the lay teams in our church, our advisory team and finance team. I could have "delegated" this one. However, I feel called to personally disciple and invest in the top tier of leaders in our church. I want their relationships with God and their families and their work to be stronger because they serve at our church at a high level.

If all of our focus is on building bigger crowds, we are simply not building the church. Yes, Jesus attracted large crowds and taught them. However, Jesus then withdrew from the crowds and invested in leaders. He knew that spiritually mature leaders would be the key to his movement. I believe they still are.

If you examine the Gospels more closely, you will see that the focus of Jesus's ministry was on a dozen leaders. If we would follow his example, we just might see the spiritual fruit we long for.

HIS KINGDOM, NOT MINE

Perhaps the most important lesson we can glean from Jesus's disciple-making efforts had to do with his mind-set. Jesus focused on *God's* kingdom, not an *earthly* kingdom.

Almost everyone Jesus encountered tried to get his focus off the big picture of God's kingdom. Satan tried by tempting Jesus with self-preservation and fame. Peter and the disciples suggested Jesus take over Rome and rule in his rightful place on earth. The crowds tried to turn Jesus into a common magician. In spite of the distractions and temptations, he wouldn't do it! He was fully surrendered and committed to building the kingdom of God, not a little earthly following. The kingdom of God was worth infinitely more than all the accolades this world could offer Jesus. We would do well to remember that. All of us would be counted as worthier servants of God if we would stop worrying so much about building the biggest church and start focusing more on building his kingdom through our church!

If building the biggest crowd were the only measure of my success, I wouldn't want any part of vocational ministry. I surrendered to the call of ministry to win people to Jesus, to rescue the lost, and to make followers of Jesus who will do the same. I want to make disciples. I want to see people growing in their relationship with God and breaking loose from addictions. I want to see marriages healed and relationships restored. I want our people to share their faith and disciple others along the way. I want to see many people in our church going somewhere around the world to share Christ's love. I want to see new churches started out of our church. I want to be part of building his kingdom, not mine!

Jesus said that if we will focus our lives and ministries on building his kingdom, all of these other things we are worrying about will take care of themselves. "But seek first his kingdom and his righteousness, and all these things will be given to you as well" (Matt. 6:33 NIV).

INSIGHT

Tim Stevens, author of Pop Goes the Church *and executive pastor of Granger Community Church, Granger, IN*

In 1993, I experienced "church" for the first time. It wasn't the first time I went to church. No, I grew up going to church three times a week, and I even went back several more times each week to volunteer or attend classes. After graduation, I joined a national ministry and worked in more than one thousand churches over the next nine years. So I was used to church.

But each of those churches was built around the "already convinced." They studied the Bible, confessed their sins to each other, met regularly, and told stories about life before meeting Jesus. It was good, but there was little *new life*. And it bothered me.

In 1993, I was invited to attend a little church in northern Indiana, about twenty minutes from my house. I resisted for months—I didn't need to see one more church. But after my first visit, I knew my life had changed. It was my first experience with the way church is supposed to be. On my first visit, I met people who had been Christians for years, others who were brand-new in their faith, and even a couple who were still kicking the tires. All in the same church on Sunday morning.

A few weeks later, I went to the church's baptism celebration at a nearby lake and watched as over fifty men and women proclaimed their faith. I thought, *Wait. These are brand-new followers of Jesus in a church of no more than three hundred people. How is that possible?*

Not long after that, I attended a men's retreat and listened to businessmen tell about how they were going to start living for Jesus instead of for themselves. I watched a guy with more tattoos than fingers and toes talk about his new decision to be a man who follows after God. And I heard many men talk about meeting Jesus and taking their first steps in this church.

A year later I joined the staff at that church, and just recently I passed my seventeen-year anniversary as one of the pastors. What is happening now? Just two months ago we baptized 457 men and women who were going public about their new faith in Jesus. The adventure continues.

I'll admit—it gets more difficult every year to keep the focus on building a flock rather than swapping sheep. Every few months I have conversations with some of the sheep who have hopped the fence to join our church, and they say things like "We need to go deeper!" or "It's too chaotic to have so many new people around here."

I choose the chaos.

New believers have their own ideas, thoughts, schedules, levels of commitment, piles of baggage from their pasts, styles of relating, opinions, and idiosyncrasies. It can be very chaotic. They don't know when to stand or sit or what to do when the person next to them at church hands them a plate full of money.

Let me encourage you to embrace the chaos. It is exactly what God has called you to. If you wish too much for the serenity of silence and chaos-free living, you may just get what you want. And then you'll find yourself in a dying church whose sole purpose is preservation rather than transformation. And trust me, that's not a fun place to be.

QUESTIONS FOR MEASUREMENT

1. What is the most challenging section of this chapter for you personally? What is the most encouraging?

2. Do you think your church leadership understands discipleship? Why or why not?

3. What are some ways your church could heighten your capacity for making disciples?

10

DO WE NEED
SOMETHING NEW?

A CALL FOR A NEW REFORMATION

think the first decade of the new millennium will be marked
as the decade when the church experienced radical change across
the world. Some might even call it one of the most innovative
decades in the history of the church. Contemporary churches
seem to be growing across our country at an incredible pace.
Innovative ideas to attract skeptics to our churches and to show
the Bible's relevance to our lives have been at the core of this
movement. But did you know that, statistically speaking, we
have not made much of a dent in the unchurched population?
It's true. Evidently, contemporary music, casual dress, coffee,
video screens, and productions complete with theatrical lighting are not going to solve all of our problems. The harvest is as
ready as it has ever been.

In fact, with my unchurched friends, there almost seems to be a new aversion to some of the slickest marketing and most innovative technology being utilized in many churches these days. The question our church began asking a couple of years ago, as we prepared for our church's second decade of ministry, is this: Does the church need something new or something old?

The Reformation is a great example of what I'm talking about. The Reformation was not a new idea. It was called the Reformation because it sought to re-form Christians and churches around what had been forgotten: God's Word. *Sola scriptura*—by Scripture alone—was the cry of the day. The Reformation was a return to Scripture as the source for faith and practice.

Should *sola scriptura* include the practices within the church? Should we desire to look more like the churches in the New Testament than the churches around the corner? I do. At least I do now. Over the last couple of years, I have led our church to do some soul searching and subsequently some repenting. There have been times when we have desired innovation over reformation. There have been times when we have tried to be too cute for our own good, when remaining "cutting-edge" dominated many of our staff discussions.

I'm afraid I'm not the only one. I think that in our desire for innovation (something new), many churches and leaders have neglected our need for reformation (something old). I'm seeing the same need in many of the most innovative churches across our nation that I saw in my own: a need for a new reformation for Christ followers and churches. At the very least, our innovation should have more to do with reformation than technology.

To be fair, innovation is not bad. Technology, lighting, video, and effects can enhance an environment for learning. Technology has afforded us the ability to cast our nets wide as we tell the Good News. As with anything else, however, we have the potential to forget the "why" behind the "what," which means we might spend more time focusing on the quality of the production than on the effectiveness of the story. And to some, the über-slick production seems a little less than sincere.

All of this is why at our church these days we are going more old school, even anti-slick. We are spending less time combing websites, blogs, and conferences for the most innovative ministry trends. Instead, we are looking to the New Testament as the guide for how we program and structure our ministries. 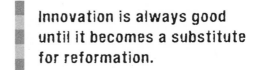 **Innovation is always good until it becomes a substitute for reformation.** We are talking less about marketing and more about how we can help our church members be the missionaries they should be.

Have we abandoned relevant evangelism? No! We are as focused as ever on reaching out to our community. Have we abandoned inviting people to our church services and utilizing practical message series? No. Have we abandoned innovation and technology? No. I'm not saying that there's anything wrong with innovation. Our church is still using technology and contemporary methods to take the gospel into our community. Creativity just doesn't drive our discussions anymore.

Innovation is always good until it becomes a substitute for reformation. If and when that happens, we need to repent. We need to daily re-form our hearts, lives, and churches around God's dream for us expressed through the New Testament, and we never need to exchange something new for something old.

Maybe one of the reasons pastors feel so unsuccessful these days is because we are trying to build something Jesus never asked us to build! When we operate outside his intention for the church and for our lives long enough, we will get frustrated as we continually work against the grain. Our spiritual energy will drain quickly. Have you ever wondered why all the budgets, hirings, firings, and constant church activities drain you? What if you're not supposed to be doing any of these things? For me, even the unceasing grind of producing an exegetical, impactful, engaging, creative, life-changing sermon every seven days is a heavy cross to bear, if not a thorn in my flesh! But where in the New Testament does it say that church has to be done this way? What if there's another way?

For the last three years, I have been part of a group of ten senior pastors from all across America who have been envisioning the "future" of the church. We call ourselves Future Travelers. This group represents over 80,000 congregants, and all of the pastors represent or work within various church networks and denominations. We have spent dozens if not hundreds of hours at this point talking about what the church should look like in the future. We have discussed in great detail this trending term called "missional communities." In one meeting, we defined missional communities this way: "reproducing groups of people who are living out the mission of Jesus in their communities." Honestly, however, this definition doesn't sound "new" to me. It sounds very old. Like two thousand years old.

We are all honest enough to admit to each other that this definition does not presently describe our big churches. So what are we doing about that? First, we are repenting. Second, we are talking, collaborating, and creating research and development departments in our churches that are more freely experimenting with various missional, incarnational approaches to ministry within our megachurches.

Our prediction is that the ideas in resources like *The Forgotten Ways* by Alan Hirsch, *On the Verge* by Alan Hirsch and Dave Ferguson, and *Launching Missional Communities* by Mike Breen and Alex Absalom are not going away. They will become even more prominent in the days to come as churches seek out new measures of success in their ministries. More churches like Austin Stone in Austin, Texas; Seacoast Church in Mount Pleasant, South Carolina; and my own church, Mountain Lake in Cumming, Georgia, will experiment with, discover, and then transition to more missional approaches to ministry. Here is another prediction: more pastors will also resign their posts from larger, more institutional churches to embark on a more missional approach to ministry. Francis Chan is one of the early examples.

I have already created a little rub by stating that I do not believe most pastors can or are supposed to lead megachurches. There are many more of us who can lead a congregation of fifty to a hundred than can lead a church staff of that size. That is just one **We might have to get comfortable with leading smaller groups of people.** reason I believe that the church must start thinking missional, multiplication, and movement more than mega and multisite.

In order for that perspective shift to occur, more of us might have to get comfortable with not being in the spotlight every seven days. We might have to get comfortable with leading smaller groups of people. We might even have to get comfortable with fading into obscurity. It might just be what liberates us from the unnecessary burdens that weigh on us. It might be what sparks a movement of God that sweeps our country and our world like the church two thousand years ago!

Make no mistake about this: these days at Mountain Lake, our innovation is about reformation. We don't need something new. We don't need a sleeker look or bigger screens. We do, however, desperately need something old, something re-formed. We need Jesus Christ and his vision for his church! Our only desire is to be successful and relevant in his eyes. We have stopped trying to be the most innovative church around, unless innovation is reformation. Interestingly enough, I think this shift is exactly what is making us one of the most relevant churches in our community again. I truly believe that in the decade to come, reformation will become innovation. If not, the church will fail to be effective in accomplishing the mission Jesus gave us. Are you troubled by that thought? I hope so.

INSIGHT

Tony Morgan, church consultant and coach
and author of TonyMorganLive.com

"And" instead of "or."

Why does it have to be attractional or missional? I've seen lives impacted by both approaches. Why can't it be attractional and missional?

Why does it have to be evangelism or discipleship? Christ followers need to be engaged in both. Why can't it be evangelism and discipleship?

Why does it have to be teaching from the platform or teaching in the living room? I've been stretched by God's Word in both settings. Why can't it be teaching from the platform and in the living room?

Why does it have to be worship with an amazing production or simple, stripped-down worship? I've experienced powerful worship in both environments. Why can't we do both?

Why does it have to be corporate gatherings or one-on-one relationships? I need to be encouraged and stretched both in my faith and in my leadership. Why can't we embrace both ways of connecting with others?

One of the things that most frustrates me about books I read about church ministry is the "or" approach they take. I don't get it. It's probably one of the reasons why in most cases I'd prefer to read marketplace books. In marketplace writing, if someone thinks they have the "right way" of doing something, they just go do it. Then they write about how it worked or didn't work. In church writing, if someone thinks they have the right way of doing something, they write about how the other church is wrong.

What if we took the "and" approach? What if we were open to the possibility that more people might be reached if we stopped doing either/or and started embracing both/and? What if God really designed some churches to be one way for one community or culture and other churches to be another way for another community or culture? My guess, as an example, is that it's going to take a completely different type of church to reach the inner city than it's going to take to reach the suburban neighborhoods of Paulding County, Georgia.

We spend a lot of time and energy fighting for the "or." I wonder what would happen if we just embraced the "and" needed to reach our communities?

The problem, of course, is that we like to worship our methods. Our preferences are the priority. In fact, we shape religion around our preferences even if it means sacrificing the broader impact of our ministry. Why help other people when it might make us uncomfortable?

I'm more of an "and" type of guy. I know that frustrates you. It would be a lot easier to dislike me if I didn't agree with you. The problem is that in many circumstances, I think you're right. The only difference is that I don't think you're always right.

And neither am I.

QUESTIONS FOR MEASUREMENT

1. In what ways are you most tempted toward the latest trends in ministry?

2. Why do you think we are so tempted to adopt the newest trends in ministry?

3. How can conferences be dangerous in this department?

4. How do we manage the tension between leveraging new technology and clinging to the timeless truths of God's Word?

11

THE CHURCH
IS NOT **THE HOPE**
OF THE WORLD

CHRISTOLOGY BEFORE ECCLESIOLOGY

I believe I first heard Bill Hybels say it: "The church is the hope of the world." I have read it in many books too. I have actually repeated it and advocated it as a mantra many times myself. However, in recent years, I have had a change of heart. I simply no longer believe it's true. I do not believe the church is the hope of the world. Yes, Jesus said, "I will build my church, and the gates of Hades will not overcome it," but he also said, "On this rock *I* will build *my* church" (Matt. 16:18 NIV, emphasis added).

In other words, the church is not the hope of the world. *Jesus* is the hope of the world. He has simply chosen to extend hope through his people, the church. Without Jesus, the church has nothing to offer anyone. Jesus is the chief cornerstone of the church. Without the cornerstone in place, the house falls. For a church to be effective, Jesus must be at the center of it. Jesus said, "I am the vine; you are the branches. Those who remain in me, and I in them, will produce much fruit. For apart from me you can do nothing" (John 15:5).

Did you catch that? The church can do *nothing* apart from Jesus living through us. We might have crowds. We might have influence. We might make a lot of noise. We might have tons of religious activity going on. We might come together for services every few days. However, Jesus said that apart from him, no long-term spiritual fruit will be produced. Apart from Jesus, we've got nothing. That's what he said!

Some of you might think that what I am saying is semantics. You may even be thinking that to make much of the church is to make much of Jesus. Not necessarily. Several years ago, we asked one of our church-planting residents to attend the worship services at one of the "hottest" church plants in the country. It was growing by leaps and bounds, and

> **Without the cornerstone in place, the house falls.**

the church and the pastor were being talked up in the religious world. Our goal was to allow our church-planting resident to learn from this young church plant with some dynamic take-aways that might assist him on his leadership journey.

When he returned from his visit, we debriefed him about his weekend. His feedback went something like this: "The parking lot was full of parking lot attendants who were friendly and spot-on with the parking logistics. The greeters were totally prepared and very helpful. The children's ministry was flat-out awesome! They had portable set designs and great actors on the stage. The worship band was really good. They had portable intelligent lighting and were kicking off a new series that was relevant to the crowd. The pastor was an amazing communicator, and he's hilarious! All in all, it was a great service. I would probably go back myself!"

At this point we turned and asked the resident, "So tell us, where was Jesus lifted up in the service?" All of a sudden our young church planter wannabe's facial expression changed. He thought for a moment and began to look down at the floor. When he looked up, tears were running down his **The church without Jesus is a cult. Period.** face. I'll never forget what he said next: "It actually just hit me. I don't think I heard his name even mentioned."

The church is not the hope of the world. In fact, the church is not even the church unless Jesus is living in and through it! The church without Jesus is a cult. Period.

It's *not* just about the weekend, stupid. Nothing could be further from the truth. If we really believed that Jesus was the hope of the world, our lives and ministries would look much different during the week. If we really believed that Jesus was the hope of the world, we as pastors would spend more time with him. By our actions, most of us prove that we actually believe our music, preaching, programs, productions, and even meetings produce more life change than prayer.

If we truly believed that Jesus was the hope of the world, he would certainly be more central to our teachings. Listen to your average sermon at your average church from your average preacher. You will no doubt hear inspiration, creativity, humor, passion, and conviction. You may or may not hear Jesus's name so much.

One congregant who recently moved to our city after attending one of the largest, most influential churches in America said to me, "I want to thank you for teaching us the Bible here. All of the teachers at [the previous church] had gotten so bad about using a verse as a diving board into a creative sermon and never coming back to God's Word." Is that an accurate statement? Probably not. But it was his opinion, his perspective of the preaching he had heard. God used this as just another reminder to me of Paul's admonition: "Preach the word of God. Be prepared, whether the time is favorable or not. Patiently correct, rebuke, and encourage your people with good teaching" (2 Tim. 4:2).

Pastors, we generally need to talk less about the church and more about Jesus. Hope will never come from creativity, anecdotes, and illustrations. Hope won't be extended through our own vision for the church. Hope will never come from an institution or even a group of people. Hope comes from the one who gave us the mission! Our churches are simply the vessel Jesus has chosen to use. The church is not the hope of the world. Jesus is the hope of the world. Jesus is the only Good News.

If we really believed Jesus was the hope of the world, our schedules and social networks would certainly look different. Too many pastors I know get so caught up feeding the ninety-nine that we don't have enough margin in our lives to go after the one. Many pastors I know teach relational evangelism but don't have a single friend who doesn't know Jesus. That bothers me. That shames me.

Since we started Mountain Lake, I have made it a practice to build enough margin in my life to connect with those disconnected from Christ and the church. I have been a part of the Chamber of Commerce, served on committees, held various board appointments, and participated in other civic service groups. Although I push my team to be highly invested in our community, I have actually taken it as a personal challenge to be more missionally engaged than any other pastor on my team. What saddens me, however, is that after serving in our community for over a decade now, I have only bumped into a couple of other pastors who were attempting to do the same thing I was—being missional. Most pastors are too busy minding their flocks. How could that happen unless we have lots of pastors who don't believe that Jesus is our community's only hope but rather think that the church is? I shudder at the thought, and it must break God's heart.

We must repent. We must change the way we think. We must change the measure of our success. We must change the direction of our lives, ministries, and churches. We must lead people to believe that our church is not the answer. We must proclaim by our actions, our teaching, and our schedules that Jesus is the only answer. Jesus is the only hope. People in our churches must become convinced of the gravity of the situation—that people who don't know Jesus

Many pastors I know teach relational evangelism but don't have a single friend who doesn't know Jesus.

are going to hell, and in the meantime, those same people are operating in a living hell without the hope of Christ. We must return to believing that Jesus is the only hope for people, and that includes us, pastors. Success is not promoting our church. Realigning ourselves with Jesus and not our own efforts should be the measure of our success.

INSIGHT

Pete Wilson, author of Plan B *and senior pastor of Cross Point Church, Nashville, TN*

Do you feel like you just got slapped in the face? That's how I felt after I finished this chapter. Shawn brought some much-needed conviction to my life and ministry.

Shawn wrote, "However, Jesus said that apart from him, no long-term spiritual fruit will be produced. Apart from Jesus, we've got nothing. That's what he said!" Those words bounced around in my head for several days.

I realize that for decades now we've been telling people in our churches that there is a simple routine to becoming more Christlike.

Go to church.

Be in a Sunday school class or small group.

Serve in children's ministry or sing in the choir.

Listen to Christian music.

Buy a Christian book.

Wear the latest Christian shirt.

Join the women's ministry.

Now, while I obviously know that God can powerfully work through these programs and institutions, I would challenge you to look around at the average Christian today.

Does the body of Christ resemble Jesus?

Well, does it?

No. Few if any studies out there reveal any kind of discernible differences between Christians and the rest of the population.

For all the focused effort religion has put on behavioral modification, it seems that very little has actually been modified. Very little sustained life change is occurring.

So maybe there's a different way.

Jesus said in John 15:4–5, "Remain in me, as I also remain in you. No branch can bear fruit by itself; it must remain in the vine. Neither can you bear fruit unless you remain in me. I am the vine; you are the branches. If you remain in me and I in you, you will bear much fruit; apart from me you can do nothing" (NIV).

There's just one thing a branch is supposed to do. Did you catch the word that kept coming up? *Remain.* I love the older translation of this word: *abide.*

I believe our job as pastors is not to develop people who are more and more committed to the church. Our job is to help people, from one moment to the next, to keep receiving this unceasing flow of life and nourishment and love from Jesus. And if your church learns to abide, or remain, the fruit will come. But if we don't stay plugged in, if we allow our lives and our ministries to be dominated by the noise and directed by the busyness, transformation will never happen, and we will never become the men and women God had in mind when he thought us into existence.

QUESTIONS FOR MEASUREMENT

1. How central would you say Jesus is to your church? Put another way, how central is Jesus in your advertising? Children's ministry? Student ministry? Worship songs? Scripture teaching?

2. How do you think your church could make Jesus and his gospel more central to everything you are and do?

12

MY RESIGNATION

STEPPING DOWN AS THE LEADER

After much prayer and reflection, I have made a private decision that I need to make public here today. Effective immediately, I am resigning as the leader of our church. Why am I taking this drastic measure? The answer is simple: the challenges of leadership here are simply more than I can currently handle. It is difficult for me to admit, but I have been in over my head for some time now. I am inadequate to lead this church. I simply cannot do it alone or be in charge anymore. I have just been unable to admit it before now. For a long time, I have carried the burden, the decisions, the pain, and the weight of trying to lead this church to greatness. I am simply incapable of accomplishing this great task.

I thought for a long time I could do it. I thought for a long time I could turn it around. I thought for a long time that I could help our church grow and reach more people. I thought I was capable of leading our team and our leaders in accomplishing our mission. I have worked hard to discipline and grow myself as a leader, preacher, and visionary for our church. More so than ever before, however, God has shown me that I am not the man for this job. That's why I have made the decision to resign.

What will I do? I'm not certain. I've always been so sure of what the next step should be for my life and ministry, but now I am not. I have always been able to think on my feet and make decisions quickly. I have long considered myself a decisive person. I have always seemed to know what to do next. I have always seemed to know how to grow our church and make disciples. Today I do not. Although I have always considered myself a good leader, especially in the church, today I do not.

What does my resignation mean for this church? Well, frankly, it means things will soon get better around here. Things will get healthier around here. This church can now return its focus to what God has called it to be and do. The church will be more unified and more loving without me in charge. The church will also possess much more ability than I can contribute to it. I am just sorry it has taken this long to come to this point.

All that being said, I have no plans to leave the church unless our members feel it is better I leave altogether. I just don't want to be the leader anymore. My plan is to continue to serve here. I may not be as visible, but I will be here. Don't be alarmed by this course of action. When new leadership is securely in place, I will follow his leadership.

In fact, I have no intention of resigning from my actual position as lead pastor of our church. I am confident that God called me here for a purpose. I have never asked him for certainty of success, just certainty of the call. I know that for now, God has called me to be lead pastor of this church. Therefore, I am not resigning from that position.

I am simply giving up any desire to be *the leader* of this church. That is not the same thing as lead pastor, nor is it my

rightful place. Jesus is the Chief Shepherd, and I am accountable to live under *his* authority and care for *his* flock. I confess
to you that this has often not been the case. I have usurped his
authority. I have disobeyed his
direct commands. I have often
done what I wanted to do at the
expense of what he has told me
to do. I have even led our church
to do things at my bidding and
led you to believe that it was his

**Together we can hold
each other accountable
for allowing Jesus to
remain the leader of
the church.**

bidding. I've never done this blatantly, but upon reflection, I
realize that the battle between my flesh and his Spirit has cost
our church at times. For that, I am sorry. I have repented to God.
Today I repent to you.

I have now accepted the fact that if our church is ever going
to become what God wants it to be, I'm going to need to de-
crease and he is going to need to increase. I'm going to need
to lead less and follow him more. In fact, I do not need to lead
the church at all. That is his job. God forbid I ever attempt to
take his place again.

Caution: this will not be my last resignation. My tendency
will be to try to take over God's role in our church from time
to time. I will both consciously and unconsciously try to steal
his glory and his position again. If you see that happening from
your perspective, I am giving you permission—in fact, I am
challenging you—to confront me and speak the truth in love
to me. I promise not to get defensive if I know that your love
for Jesus, your commitment to his mission, and your love for
me are your motives in approaching me. Together we can hold
each other accountable for allowing Jesus to remain the leader
of the church.

In fact, I think it will be important for all of us to remember that Jesus is the leader of our church. None of us are the
leaders. I would be remiss if I didn't remind us all that no

matter how long we have been at our churches or how long we have been Christians, none of us deserve to be in charge of Christ's church. Honestly, there are some among us who think they are. Others of us wish we were at times. For that, all of us need to repent.

My resignation should serve as notice that every single church leader who calls our church home needs to tender their resignations as well. None of us have a right to lead this church. None of us can hold on to leadership if we want our church to be successful. We all must resign from leadership.

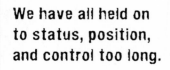

We have all held on to status, position, and control too long.

So today I am resigning my agenda. I am letting go of my selfish ambitions. I am giving up my desires. I am decreasing that he may increase. I am dying that he might live. Today I actually made the audacious request to him that he come and work through me again. I asked him to take over this church again.

Just so you know, I plan to make my resignation a way of life around here. In fact, I plan to make resignations a way of life in our church. We have all held on to status, position, and control too long. This is not our church. It belongs to Jesus. We all will resign regularly as long as I am the lead pastor.

If this decision makes you uncomfortable or even angry, I apologize for that. But that won't change my decision. I am not here to please or serve you. I am here to serve my Lord and Savior Jesus Christ, who died for me. He is the only one who has ever done this for me. He also lives for me and lives in me. He has told me that I can do all things through him and that he will strengthen me and empower me to do everything he wants me to do. He is the only one who has made that promise to me, and he is the only one who can fulfill it. From this day forward, my allegiance is to him. For our church to be successful, every one of us will need to express this same allegiance. If this scares you, you are not alone. I am scared to death. Faith is not the absence of fear. Faith is doing what God has called us to do even when we are scared.

If it is your desire to resign with me today, I want to encourage you by telling you that every time I resign, an amazing transformation happens in my life. I feel liberated. My burdens feel light. I feel an incredible sense of relief. I feel relieved to know that I don't have to be the change agent for people. I don't have to make things happen through brilliant strategy or clever preaching. Life change and church growth are God's job. I wish I had never tried to take it away from him! I feel relieved to know that I don't have to envision the future for our church. That's his job, and I'm sorry I ever tried to take that role away from him as well. I have resigned from all of it.

If by chance you are inclined to join me in resigning today, know that this will be the most difficult decision you will ever make. Saying you resign seems so easy, but it is the most difficult thing we will ever do in our lives or ministries. Fighting against our own desires and plans is always the toughest battle, isn't it? That's why, even though I had done so before privately, today I am resigning publicly. That requires some humility, but I know that public confession leads to healing and accountability. I'll keep on resigning too. Why? So God can do immeasur-

> **Life change and church growth are God's job.**

ably more than I could ever ask or imagine, and build his church *through* me. If that sounds desirable to you, would you join me in tendering your resignation today?

INSIGHT

*Brian Bloye, founder and lead pastor
of West Ridge Church, Hiram, GA*

Several years ago I was having a conversation with a close friend of mine about some of the challenges associated with being a pastor. After several minutes of conversing, he asked me a very simple but extremely profound question: "Is Jesus enough?" His question actually caught me off guard, so I asked him to elaborate. He said, "Take away the church, the title of lead pastor, the chance to influence others, and the opportunities you have been given to speak and write—is Jesus enough?" My initial response was, "Yes, I truly believe Jesus is enough." However, over the years, I've gone back to that conversation many times and replayed that question in my mind over and over. Is Jesus enough? Could I actually resign from West Ridge Church, step away from leadership, take off the hat of being a pastor, let it all go, and be satisfied that simply knowing Jesus as Lord and Savior of my life was enough to feel significant, approved, and affirmed?

Recently I read a book that addressed this issue and had a great impact on my life, Tullian Tchividjian's *Jesus + Nothing = Everything*. In a very forthright, authentic manner, Tchividjian tackles the issue that most Christians face of trying to add something to Jesus to feel worthy and approved by God. Tchividjian writes, "*Christianity and . . .* For many of us, it may be Jesus and our achievements, Jesus and our strengths, Jesus and our reputations, Jesus and our family's prosperity, Jesus and our ambitions and goals and dreams, Jesus and our personal preferences and tastes and styles, Jesus and our spiritual growth, Jesus and our hobbies and recreational pursuits and entertainment habits—and, especially, Jesus and our personal set of life rules." He then quotes Martin Luther, " 'Whatever your heart clings to and confides in, that is really your God'—your functional Savior."[1]

I would love to tell you that after nearly a quarter century of being in full-time ministry, I have this issue mastered and all figured out, but I don't. Every day I have to remind myself that when Jesus said, "It is finished" (John 19:30), he meant it. I don't have to have any add-ons to Jesus's finished work on the cross. I don't have to build my identity on anything besides God. I don't have to replace the gospel. Every day I can take off the hat of pastor, leader, shepherd, coach, husband, dad, or whatever other title I may find my identity in at the moment, and I can lay it down at the foot of the cross and find everything I need in Jesus. Jesus is truly enough.

In the book of Colossians, the apostle Paul reminds us that in Christ "are hidden all the treasures of wisdom and knowledge," "in Christ all the fullness of the Deity lives in bodily form," and "Christ is all" (2:3, 9; 3:11 NIV). Jesus Christ is all—all that I need.

QUESTIONS FOR MEASUREMENT

1. How does this chapter challenge you? How does it encourage you?

2. What do you think of this statement: "Life change and church growth are God's job."

3. In what ways are you tempted to forget that Jesus is Lord (leader) of your church?

13

THE END AND THE BEGINNING

Success. We all want it, and we all find ways to determine if we have it. Whether it's growth, numbers, fame, approval, affirmation, buzz, accolades, or just attention, every human being is tempted to measure our success by these standard measurements. Pastors and ministry leaders are no different. As a matter of fact, our success, spiritually speaking, is critical! However, our definition of success must match God's definition. Otherwise we have failed miserably.

We have been tasked by our heavenly Father to shepherd his church. He has chosen us to teach his Word, to reach out to the lost, and to challenge others to obey him. He has given us a great honor to bear such responsibility. Success for us is to remain faithful to his call and giftings. We cannot—we must not—take our eyes off the goal. The kingdom of heaven cannot afford for us to seek success in any other way.

We must not seek to please people. We must please God.

We must not seek to fill auditoriums. We must fill heaven.

We must not seek fame. We must make Jesus famous.

We must not seek our agenda. We must proclaim his agenda.

We must not quit if we are called. We will quit if we are not.

The measure of our success is clear. It is laid out for us in Scripture. If we muddy the waters with our own desires and expectations, we will ultimately fail in the very thing we have given our lives to: our ministries.

The battle for our hearts and minds is great. We must not succumb to the temptation to do anything for anyone other than what our God has commanded. Our success is not measured by our roller coaster of emotions or the flippant opinions of others. Our success is measured only by the one who called us. Is that enough for you? My prayer for this work has been that this goal would become the measure of your success. If it does, this work will have been worth it.

We must not succumb to the temptation to do anything for anyone other than what our God has commanded.

INSIGHT

Dr. Samuel R. Chand, author
of Cracking Your Church's Culture Code

In my leadership consultations, regardless of how the issues are framed, the bottom-line question is, "How can I be *more* successful?" Rarely do I have someone admitting failure; rather it is about being *more* successful. That assumes a measure of success, however that is defined in the life and organization of the leader. The emphasis is on *more*.

Existential questions always intrigue me. "What's *more* all about? Why do we always yearn for *more?* What is *enough?* Will *more* bring me fulfillment?" I'll let people wiser than me answer those questions. Let me wrestle not with the answer but rather with the existential angst of it all.

Little kids cry and whine for *more*. Later we learn to manipulate for *more*. Then we pretend we have *more*. We—yes, Christian leaders—lie about *more*. Finding actual and honest numbers of people in attendance, income, expenses, staff members, ministries, and volunteers becomes a game of smoke and mirrors. We don't want anyone to know the truth because we want them to have the illusion that we have *more*.

Yes, I've been through it all. As a youth pastor, then a lead pastor, then a Christian university president, and now with consulting and speaking clientele, the quest for *more* continued . . .

Until I realized that *more* was a mirage that drew me deeper into the desert by giving me the illusion that there is water ahead, and I was reminded of Jeremiah 2:13: "For my people have committed two evils; they have forsaken me the fountain of living waters, and hewed them out cisterns, broken cisterns, that can hold no water" (KJV).

Or as *The Message* says it, "My people have committed a compound sin: they've walked out on me, the fountain of fresh flowing waters, and then dug cisterns—cisterns that leak, cisterns that are no better than sieves."

When I realized that my *more* can only be satisfied in, by, and through the Lord, the struggle intensified even greater! It is easier to go for *more* on my own than to let him be the *more* in my life.

I wish I could end this section by giving you a superbly glorious testimony of sorts, but rather I want to acknowledge that I'm a fellow struggler in this leadership pilgrimage, trying to win the battle over *more*.

NOTES

Chapter 1 What's Wrong with Pastors?

1. Ed Stetzer, "7 Issues Church Planters Face, Issue #7: Spiritual, Physical and Mental Health of Planter/Family," *Ed Stetzer: The Lifeway Research Blog,* February 4, 2011, http://www.edstetzer.com/2011/02/7-top-issues-church-planters-f-4.html#more. Ed Stetzer's research with Todd Wilson, founder of the Exponential conference, was presented on Ed's blog as well at our Velocity conference in February 2011 and at the Exponential conference this past year.

Chapter 6 Success Is Spelled TEAM

1. John Maxwell, *The 21 Irrefutable Laws of Leadership: Follow Them and People Will Follow You* (Nashville: Thomas Nelson, 1998), 20.

2. Samuel R. Chand, *Cracking Your Church's Culture Code: Seven Keys to Unleashing Vision and Inspiration* (San Francisco: Jossey-Bass, 2011), 173.

Chapter 7 Prophecy, Criticism, and Success

1. Bill Hybels, *Axiom: Powerful Leadership Proverbs* (Grand Rapids: Zondervan, 2008), 159.

2. C. H. Spurgeon, *Letters to My Students* (London: Paternoster, 1877), 134.

Chapter 9 Measuring What Matters

1. Larry Osborne, *Sticky Church* (Grand Rapids: Zondervan, 2008).

Chapter 12 My Resignation

1. Tullian Tchividjian, *Jesus + Nothing = Everything* (Wheaton: Crossway, 2011), 39–40.

Shawn Lovejoy is the founding and lead pastor of Mountain Lake Church and the directional leader of Churchplanters.com. God has led Mountain Lake Church and Churchplanters.com to become one of the most influential church planting ministries in the world, and Shawn gives Jesus all the credit. Shawn loves his wife, his kids, the church, pastors, college football, and PlayStation 3, in that order. He lives near Atlanta, Georgia.

COACHING
LEADERS FOR
GREATER IMPACT

CHURCHPLANTERS.COM
giving you permission

Check out Churchplanters.com for free resources including:
series and graphic downloads, online coaching and networking, and
daily blog posts from ministry leaders addressing issues we face every day.

Stay Connected

Shawn loves connecting with ministry leaders
and he has a passion for pastoring pastors.

Stay Connected for:

- Leadership and Coaching Tips
- Personal and Spiritual Growth Lessons
- Ministry Techniques and Tools
- Networking amongst Top Ministry Leaders
- Free Resources to Help Your Church Grow
- Updates on Latest Ministry Trends

Twitter: @shawnlovejoy
Facebook: Shawn Lovejoy
Blog: www.shawnlovejoy.com